LUNA NIGHTINGALE

Smart Saving

The Ultimate Guide To Saving Money And Building Wealth

GOLDEN LEAF
HAVEN
PUBLISHING

First published by Golden Leaf Haven Publishing 2025

Golden Leaf Haven Publishing, 36 Saint John's Place, Freeport 11520-4618, New York, USA

Airhub 1425, UBX 6 Poyle Trading Estate, Colndale Road, Colnbrook, Slough SL30AA Berkshire, United Kingdom

First edition

Contents

Introduction

The Importance of Saving Money

In today's fast-paced world, the significance of saving money cannot be overstated. Whether it's for short-term goals such as purchasing a new gadget, or for long-term aspirations like securing a comfortable retirement, having a solid savings plan is key to achieving financial stability and peace of mind. Many individuals live paycheck to paycheck, often unaware of the power that saving money consistently can bring. Saving is not just about putting money aside for a rainy day, it's about creating opportunities for financial freedom and security.

In this modern age, it's easy to get caught up in consumerism and the pressures of instant gratification. With credit cards, loans, and easy access to financing, it's tempting to spend now and worry about the future later. However, the truth is, financial problems can arise at any moment. Medical emergencies, unexpected home repairs, or job loss can shake our financial foundations. By learning the importance of saving and taking action to build up a reserve of funds, we can weather these unexpected events and navigate them without stress or fear.

Saving money is also a means of taking control over your financial future. It's about building a cushion that empowers you to make decisions based on what's best for you, rather than reacting to financial constraints. Having savings gives you the flexibility to pursue dreams, take career risks, travel, or invest in experiences that enrich your life.

This book will help you understand why saving money is so crucial, and more importantly, how to start saving effectively—no matter your income level. Whether you are just starting your savings journey or looking for new strategies to optimize your savings, the steps outlined in this guide will provide the tools you need to begin your path toward financial independence.

Why Saving Is Essential for Financial Security

Saving money is often regarded as one of the most fundamental aspects of achieving financial security. Whether you're working toward a comfortable retirement, preparing for unexpected expenses, or simply trying to build wealth, saving plays a pivotal role in achieving your financial goals. But why is saving so essential, and how does it contribute to financial security? In this article, we'll explore the many reasons why saving money is not just a good idea, but a critical component of financial health.

1. Building an Emergency Fund

One of the most immediate benefits of saving is the ability to create an emergency fund. Life is unpredictable, and emergencies such as medical bills, car repairs, or job loss can occur at any time. An emergency fund acts as a financial cushion that provides you with the means to cover these unexpected expenses without going into debt.

Without adequate savings, you may find yourself relying on credit cards or loans to cover emergencies, which can lead to financial instability. An emergency fund, typically recommended to cover three to six months' worth of living expenses, is a fundamental step in protecting yourself from financial setbacks.

2. Avoiding Debt and Interest Payments

When you save money, you reduce your reliance on credit. High-interest debt—such as credit card balances, payday loans, or personal loans—can quickly spiral out of control and consume a significant portion of your income. By saving, you lower the likelihood that you'll need to take on debt for everyday expenses or emergency situations.

When you're not borrowing, you avoid paying high interest rates on loans. Over time, interest can accumulate, and you'll end up paying much more than what you initially borrowed. Saving allows you to bypass this cycle of debt and interest payments, freeing up money that can be better used for other financial goals.

3. Achieving Long-Term Financial Goals

Financial goals—whether it's buying a home, starting a business, funding a child's education, or traveling the world—require careful planning and financial discipline. Saving is the first step in making these long-term goals achievable. By setting aside money each month, you are working toward building the financial resources needed to meet these aspirations.

For example, buying a home typically requires a substantial down payment. The more money you save, the easier it will be to secure a mortgage with favorable terms. Similarly, saving for retirement ensures that you have the funds necessary to live comfortably after you stop working. Building up your savings gives you the financial flexibility and stability to pursue your long-term dreams without relying on external financial support.

4. Retirement Security

One of the most compelling reasons to save is the need to prepare for retirement. Many people mistakenly believe that Social Security or a pension will be enough to cover their expenses after they retire. However, for most individuals, these sources of income are insufficient to maintain their desired lifestyle. Saving for retirement ensures that you have enough funds to live comfortably when you're no longer earning a paycheck.

Retirement savings vehicles such as 401(k)s, IRAs, and other investment accounts allow you to build wealth over time, taking advantage of compound interest. The earlier you start saving, the more time your money has to grow. By saving consistently, you can accumulate the resources needed for a secure and fulfilling retirement.

5. Financial Independence and Freedom

Financial independence refers to the ability to live comfortably without having to rely on a job or outside sources of income. This level of financial security is achievable through consistent saving and smart investment strategies. Saving allows you to gain control over your financial future, giving you the option to retire early, start a business, or pursue hobbies without worrying about money.

By saving, you can develop multiple streams of income, diversify your investments, and build wealth in ways that give you freedom and flexibility. The more you save, the greater your ability to make choices based on your personal preferences rather than external financial pressures.

6. Reducing Financial Stress

Money is one of the most significant sources of stress for individuals and families. Constant worry about bills, debt, and unexpected expenses can take a toll on both mental and physical health. Saving money can alleviate much of this stress by providing a financial cushion for life's uncertainties.

Knowing that you have the financial resources to cover basic needs and emergencies gives you peace of mind. You no longer have to worry about the next paycheck or the possibility of falling into debt. Financial stability enables you to approach life with confidence, knowing that you are prepared for whatever comes your way.

7. Wealth Building and Investment Opportunities

When you save, you not only build a safety net for emergencies but also create opportunities for wealth-building. Once you have saved enough for emergencies and short-term goals, you can begin to invest. Investments, such as stocks, bonds, or real estate, allow your money to grow over time, often at a faster rate than standard savings accounts.

Through investing, your wealth can multiply, providing you with greater financial security and opportunities in the future. Saving money is the first step toward investment, as it provides the capital needed to take advantage of various investment opportunities. By regularly saving and investing, you can build wealth that will support your goals and secure your future.

8. Setting an Example for Future Generations

Saving is not only beneficial for you; it also sets a positive example for your children or younger family members. When children see their parents prioritize saving and planning for the future, they are more likely to adopt healthy financial habits of their own. Teaching the value of saving from a young age ensures that future generations are financially responsible, prepared for challenges, and able to achieve their own financial goals.

By instilling good savings habits, you help ensure that your loved ones are set up for financial success, just as you are working toward achieving financial security for yourself.

9. Protecting Against Inflation

Inflation erodes the purchasing power of money over time. Without proper savings and investments, the cost of goods and services will continue to rise, and your savings may not be enough to keep up. Saving regularly helps to protect the value of your money, especially when you invest in assets that have the potential to outpace inflation.

Inflation can erode savings held in traditional savings accounts, but investing in assets like stocks, real estate, and commodities can provide better protection against inflation's effects. By saving and investing wisely, you ensure that your wealth continues to grow and maintain its value over time.

Saving is not just a financial practice—it's a fundamental element of financial security and peace of mind. Whether you're building an emergency fund, saving for retirement, or planning for big life goals, saving money ensures that you're prepared for life's uncertainties. It reduces debt, builds wealth, and allows you to achieve financial freedom and independence. The more you save, the more opportunities you create for yourself and your loved ones, enabling you to live a stress-free and fulfilling life. Saving is an investment in your future, and it's one of the most important steps you can take toward achieving financial security and long-term success.

Common Misconceptions About Saving Money

Saving money is one of the most essential financial habits to develop, yet it often feels like a daunting task for many. Despite the growing importance of personal finance education, there are still a number of misconceptions that hinder people from building strong savings habits. These misunderstandings can prevent individuals from reaching their financial goals and can even lead them down the wrong path when it comes to managing their money.

We will explore some of the most common misconceptions about saving money and shed light on why they are misleading.

1. You Need to Earn a High Salary to Save Money

One of the most common misconceptions about saving money is that you need to earn a high income to be able to save. People often believe that only those who make a significant amount of money have the ability to put anything aside for the future. The reality is that saving money is more about habits and discipline than it is about how much you earn.

No matter how small your income may be, you can still save money if you focus on cutting unnecessary expenses, prioritizing savings, and living within your means. It's the consistency of saving, not the size of your paycheck, that makes the difference. Many people earning modest salaries are able to build significant savings by making intentional, thoughtful choices about how they manage their money.

2. I Need to Save a Large Amount of Money at Once

Another misconception is that savings must always be significant amounts. This belief can discourage many from even attempting to save because they feel they don't have enough to make a difference. The truth is that even small amounts can add up over time, and it's the habit of saving regularly that counts.

Saving small amounts consistently is often more beneficial than waiting to save a large sum. You may not have the luxury of stashing away thousands of dollars each month, but you can still save a few dollars here and there. Over time, these smaller contributions can accumulate, especially when combined with the power of compound interest.

3. You Can Only Save Money by Cutting Back on Luxuries

Many people think that saving money requires extreme frugality, such as eliminating all forms of entertainment, dining out, or purchasing luxury items. While cutting back on unnecessary expenses can help you save, it's not necessary to completely deprive yourself of the things you enjoy. In fact, the key is in finding a balance that works for you.

Instead of cutting out all pleasures, it's better to focus on prioritizing your spending. Are there smaller or less frequent indulgences that you can reduce or replace? Instead of eating out every day, perhaps try cooking more meals at home. Rather than constantly purchasing the latest gadgets, think about whether those items are truly necessary.

Living a fulfilling life while saving money isn't about eliminating joy—it's about being mindful and intentional with your choices. Budgeting allows you to enjoy the things that matter most without derailing your financial goals.

4. Saving Money Means You Can't Have Fun

A related misconception is that saving money means you must lead an austere, boring lifestyle with no room for fun or adventure. People often associate saving money with missing out on travel, entertainment, and experiences that bring joy. However, saving doesn't have to be about sacrificing everything you enjoy. It's about making choices that allow you to achieve long-term goals without feeling deprived.

There are plenty of ways to enjoy life while saving. Opt for more affordable leisure activities, such as hiking, free community events, or exploring new places close to home. Travel doesn't have to mean luxurious resorts—budget travel can be just as exciting and enriching. The key is to find a balance where your financial future is secure, but you're still able to enjoy the present.

5. I Can Start Saving Later—It's Too Late Now

Many people delay saving money, thinking it's something they can do "later" or when they have more money or when their circumstances improve. The reality is that the earlier you start saving, the more time your money has to grow. Time is one of the most powerful factors in building wealth, thanks to compound interest.

Even if you feel that you're behind or have made financial mistakes in the past, it's never too late to start saving. Whether you're in your 20s, 30s, or even 40s, beginning to save is better than never starting at all. The sooner you take control of your finances, the sooner you'll start to see the benefits.

6. Debt Means You Can't Save Money

It's a common belief that if you have debt, you can't save money. While it's crucial to prioritize paying off high-interest debts like credit card balances, this doesn't mean you should stop saving altogether. In fact, having an emergency fund in place is an essential part of financial stability, even while paying down debt.

You don't need to pay off every single debt before starting to save. You can work toward both goals simultaneously by setting aside small amounts each month for savings while tackling debt. The key is to find a strategy that works for your specific situation and maintain consistency.

7. You Need a Fancy Savings Account to Save Properly

Another misconception is that you need a special savings account or investment product to save money effectively. While certain accounts may offer higher interest rates or additional features, it's important to note that the most important aspect of saving is simply putting money aside regularly.

If you're just starting out, you can save money in a basic savings account. Once you're able to save larger amounts, you can look into options like high-yield savings accounts, certificates of deposit (CDs), or investments. But the most important step is to begin saving, no matter the vehicle you use.

8. Saving Money Requires Major Life Changes

Some people believe that saving money requires dramatic changes to their lifestyle or a complete overhaul of their financial habits. While some adjustments may be necessary, saving money doesn't have to be an overwhelming or burdensome process. Small, manageable changes to your daily habits—such as cutting back on impulse purchases or reducing subscription services you no longer use—can make a significant impact without drastically altering your way of life.

Instead of trying to implement extreme changes, focus on incremental improvements. Over time, these small shifts can lead to big results.

9. Once You Reach Your Goal, You Can Stop Saving

Another misconception is that saving is only important for a specific goal or milestone. Once you've saved enough for an emergency fund, a vacation, or retirement, you can stop saving. In reality, saving is a lifelong process. Even after reaching a goal, you should continue saving to ensure financial security for the future.

Financial circumstances can change unexpectedly—emergencies can arise, and opportunities for new investments can present themselves. Saving continually, even after you've reached one goal, provides a safety net and a means to continue building wealth.

10. Financial Advisors Are Only for the Wealthy

Lastly, some people believe that only those with significant wealth can afford a financial advisor. While wealthier individuals may benefit from the guidance of a financial expert, financial advisors are available to people of all income levels. Many offer affordable services or even free consultations, making them accessible to a wide range of clients.

If you're unsure where to begin with saving or investing, a financial advisor can help you create a plan that aligns with your goals and budget.

Saving money is an important skill that everyone should learn, but it's often clouded by misconceptions. The key to successful saving lies in understanding that it's not about how much you earn, but rather about the choices you make, the habits you develop, and the consistency with which you approach your financial goals. By addressing and dispelling these common myths, you can set yourself on a path toward a more secure and prosperous future.

The Long-Term Benefits of Starting to Save Early

Saving money is one of the most powerful steps you can take to secure your financial future. Yet, despite its importance, many people delay saving for the future. The truth is, the sooner you start saving, the better off you will be in the long run. By beginning early, you set yourself up for financial security, wealth accumulation, and peace of mind as you age. Here, we will explore the long-term benefits of starting to save early, from compound interest to financial freedom and stress reduction.

1. The Power of Compound Interest

One of the most significant advantages of starting to save early is the power of compound interest. Compound interest is the interest earned not only on the initial principal but also on the accumulated interest from previous periods. Essentially, you earn "interest on interest," and over time, this can result in exponential growth.

The earlier you start, the more time your money has to grow. Even small amounts saved early on can snowball into significant sums over the years.

2. Building Wealth Over Time

When you start saving early, you give yourself a head start on building wealth. Wealth-building isn't just about earning a high income; it's about consistently saving and investing your money over time. The sooner you begin, the more time you have to accumulate wealth.

By saving early, you can also take advantage of opportunities for higher returns in the long run. For example, by investing in the stock market, real estate, or other investment vehicles, you allow your money to grow in ways that might not be possible if you wait to start saving. Over the decades, these investments can grow substantially, giving you a much higher net worth as you age.

The longer you wait to start saving, the harder it will be to accumulate wealth because you will have fewer years for your money to grow. Starting early ensures that you are on the right path to long-term wealth.

3. Financial Security and Independence

Another significant benefit of starting to save early is the ability to achieve financial security and independence. When you save early and consistently, you create a safety net that protects you from unexpected events like job loss, medical emergencies, or other financial setbacks. You will be able to weather life's storms more easily when you have a substantial amount of savings in place.

In addition to providing a safety net, starting to save early can lead to financial independence. Financial independence means that you have enough money saved and invested so that you no longer need to rely on a paycheck to cover your living expenses. With early savings and investments, you can build a portfolio of assets that generates income, allowing you to have more control over your life.

By saving and investing early, you set yourself on the path toward financial freedom, meaning you can make decisions based on what you want rather than being bound by financial necessity.

4. Reduced Financial Stress

Financial stress is one of the leading causes of anxiety for many people. Worrying about how you will pay for retirement, cover unexpected expenses, or fund your children's education can take a significant toll on your mental and emotional health. However, when you start saving early, you relieve some of that stress by providing yourself with a cushion for the future.

The more you save and invest now, the less likely you will be to experience financial hardship down the road. Having a savings plan in place helps ensure that you are prepared for whatever comes your way. It allows you to face financial challenges with confidence, knowing that you have resources to fall back on.

In contrast, those who delay saving often feel more anxious as they age, especially when they realize they don't have enough saved for the future. This can lead to feelings of regret and fear about the future.

5. Preparing for Retirement

Retirement might seem like a distant concept when you're in your 20s or 30s, but the earlier you start saving, the easier it will be to achieve a comfortable retirement. Starting to save early gives you more time to build up the nest egg you will need to support yourself when you stop working.

If you wait until your 40s or 50s to start saving for retirement, you will likely have to save a much larger percentage of your income in order to catch up. This can be difficult if you have other financial obligations, such as a mortgage or college tuition for your children. By starting early, you give yourself the advantage of spreading out your retirement savings over many years, which makes it much easier to achieve your retirement goals.

Additionally, starting early means you can take advantage of employer-sponsored retirement accounts, such as 401(k) plans, and individual retirement accounts (IRAs). These accounts offer tax advantages and other benefits that can help your retirement savings grow faster.

6. Improved Money Habits

Starting to save early also helps you develop better money habits that will serve you well throughout your life. When you begin saving at a young age, you learn the importance of budgeting, tracking expenses, and setting financial goals. These habits become ingrained in your daily life and help you make smarter financial decisions in the future.

The discipline of saving early also helps you avoid common financial pitfalls, such as accumulating high-interest debt or living beyond your means. By developing a savings mindset, you increase your chances of financial success over time.

7. Financial Legacy for Future Generations

Finally, starting to save early not only benefits you but also helps secure the financial future of your family and future generations. When you begin saving and investing early, you can build wealth that can be passed down to your children or grandchildren. This financial legacy provides them with opportunities for education, homeownership, and other life goals that might otherwise be out of reach.

Additionally, by saving early, you may be able to leave behind a significant inheritance, which can help your loved ones build a strong financial foundation. This is a gift that keeps giving for generations to come.

The long-term benefits of starting to save early are undeniable. From harnessing the power of compound interest to building wealth, achieving financial security, reducing stress, and preparing for retirement, the earlier you start saving, the greater the rewards will be. It's never too early to begin thinking about your financial future, and by taking action now, you put yourself in a strong position to achieve your financial goals. Whether you're saving for retirement, a home, or your children's education, starting early gives you the time and resources you need to make your dreams a reality. Don't wait—take control of your financial future today.

Understanding Your Financial Situation

Before embarking on any financial journey, it's crucial to understand where you stand. Your current financial situation serves as the foundation upon which you can build your wealth, plan for your future, and secure financial independence. By assessing your financial health, you'll gain clarity on where you need to improve, where you are thriving, and where you can make adjustments to set yourself up for long-term success.

Evaluating Your Income

Start by taking a clear look at your income sources. Income is the money that you earn, whether it comes from your job, business, investments, or any other source. Track all your income streams and analyze them over time. Are they consistent, or do they fluctuate significantly from month to month? Understanding your income will help you identify patterns, areas for growth, or potential instability in your financial situation.

It's also important to understand your net income—the amount left over after taxes, insurance, and other deductions are taken out. This is the money you have available to manage your spending, savings, and investments. It's important not only to know your gross income (total income before deductions) but also your net income to have a clear picture of what you're actually working with.

Tracking Your Expenses

Next, take stock of your expenses. Start by reviewing your monthly bills, including rent/mortgage, utilities, insurance, and loan payments. Track your discretionary spending—expenses such as groceries, entertainment, dining out, and shopping. A detailed understanding of where your money is going each month can reveal areas where you might cut back or prioritize your spending.

The key is to track all expenses, even the small ones. Often, small, repeated expenses add up over time and can be a source of financial leakage that you may not realize until you take a closer look. Use budgeting tools, apps, or even a simple spreadsheet to monitor your spending patterns. This exercise will provide you with valuable insight into areas where you can reduce costs and boost savings.

Reviewing Your Debts and Liabilities

Understanding your liabilities is another crucial step in assessing your financial situation. Debts, loans, credit card balances, mortgages, and student loans are all liabilities that you need to account for. Begin by making a list of all your debts, including their interest rates and repayment schedules.

Focus on high-interest debts, as these can quickly become burdensome if not managed carefully. Prioritize paying off these types of debts to free up more money for saving and investing. For those with student loans or mortgages, try to understand the repayment terms and explore options for refinancing or consolidating if applicable.

Assessing Your Assets

Assets are anything you own that holds value and can be used to generate income or be sold for cash. Common assets include savings, investments (stocks, bonds, mutual funds), property (real estate), and even valuable items such as jewelry or collectibles.

List all your assets and estimate their current value. While your home may be one of your most significant assets, it's important to remember that assets like real estate can fluctuate in value based on market conditions. In addition to evaluating the current value of your assets, consider their potential for growth or income generation in the future. Investments like stocks or retirement accounts can provide long-term wealth accumulation, while real estate can offer opportunities for rental income or appreciation in value.

Net Worth Calculation

Once you have a comprehensive understanding of your income, expenses, debts, and assets, you can calculate your net worth. Net worth is the difference between what you own (assets) and what you owe (liabilities). To calculate your net worth:

1. Add up the value of all your assets (bank accounts, investments, property, etc.).

2. Subtract your liabilities (credit card debts, loans, mortgages, etc.).

A positive net worth means you have more assets than liabilities, which is a good sign of financial health. A negative net worth indicates that you owe more than you own, which may require you to reevaluate your financial priorities and work towards reducing debt and increasing savings.

Identifying Financial Strengths and Weaknesses

By evaluating your financial situation, you can identify your strengths and weaknesses. If you're saving more than you spend, have little or no debt, and have a strong asset base, you're in a solid financial position. However, if you find that you're spending more than you earn, carrying high-interest debt, and struggling to save or invest, you may need to take immediate steps to improve your situation.

Setting Financial Goals

The next step is to set specific, measurable financial goals. Whether your aim is to pay off debt, save for retirement, purchase a home, or build an emergency fund, having clear objectives will help you stay focused and motivated. Break your larger goals into smaller, manageable milestones, and set realistic timeframes for achieving them.

Understanding your financial situation is the first step towards gaining control over your finances and setting yourself up for long-term financial success. By assessing your income, expenses, debts, assets, and net worth, you'll have a clearer idea of where you stand and what actions you need to take to move forward on your journey to financial freedom.

Analyzing Income and Expenses

Understanding personal finances is key to achieving financial stability and success. One of the most crucial aspects of managing personal finances is the ability to analyze income and expenses effectively. This analysis provides a clear picture of your financial situation and allows you to make informed decisions, set realistic financial goals, and ultimately improve your financial health. In this article, we will explore the importance of analyzing income and expenses, how to track and assess them, and how you can use the analysis to optimize your finances.

The Importance of Analyzing Income and Expenses

Income is the money you earn from various sources, such as your salary, business profits, investments, or any other income stream. Expenses, on the other hand, represent the money you spend on goods and services, such as rent, utilities, groceries, insurance, and entertainment. The balance between your income and expenses is the foundation of your financial situation.

Analyzing income and expenses is essential because it allows you to:

1. Identify Financial Strengths and Weaknesses: By reviewing your income and expenses, you can identify areas where you are doing well financially, such as having a stable income or living within your means. Similarly, it helps you pinpoint weaknesses, such as excessive spending, inadequate savings, or high debt.

2. Create a Realistic Budget: A clear understanding of your income and expenses allows you to create a realistic budget. A budget is a plan that allocates your income to cover both essential and non-essential expenses. Without a solid understanding of your financial inflows and outflows, it is impossible to create a budget that truly reflects your financial situation.

3. Set Financial Goals: Once you know where your money is coming from and where it's going, you can set achievable financial goals. For example, you may decide to save for a down payment on a house, build an emergency fund, or pay off credit card debt. Analyzing your income and expenses helps you set realistic goals and gives you a clear path to achieving them.

4. Prevent Debt Accumulation: When you track both income and expenses, you are less likely to spend more than you earn, which prevents unnecessary debt accumulation. Understanding your spending habits can help you make better choices and avoid impulse buys that could lead to financial strain.

5. Improve Financial Decision-Making: Regular analysis of income and expenses provides you with insights that allow you to make better financial decisions. Whether it's choosing between a high-interest savings account, investing in stocks, or cutting back on discretionary spending, understanding your financial situation enables you to make well-informed choices.

How to Track and Analyze Income and Expenses

The first step in analyzing income and expenses is to gather data. You can do this manually using a spreadsheet or use financial tracking apps or software that automatically tracks and categorizes your income and spending. Here are the key steps involved:

1. Track All Sources of Income

Start by listing all your income sources. These can include:

- Primary Income: Your salary or wages, if you are employed.
- Secondary Income: Income from side gigs, freelance work, or passive income such as dividends from investments or rental income.
- One-time Income: Bonuses, gifts, tax refunds, or inheritance.

For each source of income, note the amount and the frequency (weekly, monthly, annually). This helps you see the total income that is coming in each month and gives you a clear view of your earning capacity.

2. Categorize Your Expenses

Next, list all your expenses and categorize them. It's important to differentiate between essential and non-essential expenses. Here are some common categories:

- Fixed Expenses: These are the expenses that remain constant each month, such as rent/mortgage, utilities, insurance, loan repayments, and subscriptions. Fixed expenses do not vary in amount, making them easier to track.

- Variable Expenses: These include groceries, gas, transportation, and other day-to-day expenses. These amounts can fluctuate month-to-month, so they may require more effort to track.

- Discretionary Expenses: These are non-essential items like entertainment, dining out, shopping, and vacations. These can often be adjusted or eliminated if you're trying to save more money.

Categorizing your expenses helps you identify areas where you can make adjustments. For example, reducing discretionary spending or finding ways to lower variable expenses can help you balance your budget and increase savings.

3. Review and Analyze Your Spending Habits

Once you have tracked and categorized your income and expenses, it's time to analyze them. This is where the real work begins. Consider the following:

- Income vs. Expenses: Does your income exceed your expenses, or do you spend more than you earn? If you're spending more than you earn, you may need to reevaluate your expenses or look for ways to increase your income.

- Percentage Breakdown: What percentage of your income is allocated to each expense category? For instance, the 50/30/20 rule is a popular budgeting strategy: 50% of your income should go to essentials, 30% to discretionary spending, and 20% to savings and debt repayment. You can adjust this according to your own financial priorities.

- Trends Over Time: Is your spending increasing month after month, or are there certain months where expenses spike? Analyzing trends over time can help you identify patterns and prevent future financial challenges. It could also highlight areas where you may need to reduce spending or reallocate your resources.

4. Look for Areas to Cut Back

After reviewing your income and expenses, it's time to identify areas where you can cut back. Start with discretionary spending and ask yourself:

- Do you need that extra subscription?
  - Can you cook at home more instead of eating out?
  - Are there cheaper alternatives for your utility providers?

Small adjustments can add up over time, and finding ways to cut back on unnecessary spending can free up money for savings or paying down debt.

5. Evaluate Long-Term Financial Goals

Finally, it's important to evaluate your long-term financial goals. Are you saving for a home, retirement, or your child's education? Your analysis should help you determine whether you are on track to achieve these goals or whether changes to your spending habits are needed. If you're not meeting your goals, consider reallocating money to savings and investments to increase your wealth.

Using Income and Expense Analysis to Make Better Financial Decisions

Once you have a clear understanding of your income and expenses, you can use this analysis to make informed decisions about your financial future. Here are a few ways to apply what you've learned:

- Create a Budget: Based on your analysis, create a budget that aligns with your income and expenses. A well-planned budget can help you live within your means, save for the future, and avoid debt.

- Set Realistic Financial Goals: Use the insights you've gained to set financial goals that are achievable within your income and expense limits. For example, if you're aiming to pay off debt, your goal might include reducing discretionary spending and increasing monthly debt repayments.

- Track Progress: Regularly track your income and expenses to see if you are sticking to your budget and meeting your financial goals. If you're falling behind, adjust your spending habits as needed.

- Review and Adjust: Financial situations change, so it's important to regularly review your income and expenses to ensure your budget remains relevant. If your income increases or you face new expenses, update your budget to reflect these changes.

Analyzing income and expenses is a vital practice for anyone seeking financial stability and growth. By understanding where your money comes from and where it goes, you can create a solid financial plan that helps you achieve your goals. Through regular analysis, you can avoid debt, build wealth, and maintain control over your financial future. Whether you're just starting out or looking to refine your financial habits, taking the time to track and assess your income and expenses will pay off in the long run.

Setting Up a Budget: Tracking Spending and Cutting Unnecessary Costs

Creating and sticking to a budget is an essential aspect of personal finance management that many individuals often overlook or find difficult to maintain. However, by setting up a solid budget, you can gain better control of your money, avoid overspending, and work toward financial goals like saving for the future, paying off debt, or buying a home. This guide will walk you through how to set up a budget by tracking your spending and identifying ways to cut unnecessary costs.

1. Understand Your Financial Situation

Before diving into the specifics of setting up a budget, it's important to understand where you stand financially. Take the time to analyze your income, expenses, debts, and savings. By understanding these key aspects of your financial life, you will have a clearer picture of what areas you need to focus on in your budget.

Step 1: Track Your Income

Begin by determining your monthly income. This includes your salary, any side hustles, freelance work, or passive income sources. If your income varies from month to month, calculate an average over the last few months. Be sure to account for after-tax income, as this is the actual amount you have available to spend.

Step 2: Track Your Expenses

Tracking your expenses is critical to understanding where your money is going. There are several ways to track expenses:

- Use an Expense Tracking App: Many apps are designed to automatically track your spending by syncing with your bank accounts and credit cards. Examples include Mint, YNAB (You Need A Budget), or PocketGuard.
- Manually Track Your Expenses: You can also write down your

expenses in a notebook or create a spreadsheet to log them. Make sure to categorize your spending—such as housing, transportation, groceries, utilities, entertainment, etc.

Step 3: List Your Debts and Savings Goals

Now that you have an idea of your income and expenses, it's time to focus on any debts you owe, such as credit card balances, student loans, or car loans. Additionally, list your savings goals. This might include building an emergency fund, saving for retirement, or putting money aside for a future vacation or large purchase.

2. Categorize Your Expenses

The next step in setting up your budget is categorizing your expenses. Once you've tracked your spending for at least a month, you can group your expenses into fixed and variable categories.

Fixed Expenses: These are expenses that remain relatively consistent month to month and include rent or mortgage, car payments, insurance premiums, student loans, and any other recurring bills you know are coming each month. These expenses are typically non-negotiable.

Variable Expenses: These are costs that fluctuate each month, such as groceries, utilities, gas, entertainment, dining out, and shopping. While these expenses can vary, they are usually within your control, which is why they offer the most potential for cutting unnecessary costs.

Discretionary Expenses: These are non-essential expenses, such as eating out at restaurants, entertainment, hobbies, or luxury items. While they may enhance your lifestyle, they're not necessary for survival or basic functioning.

3. Set Your Budget Categories

Once you've identified your expenses, it's time to create a plan for each category. A popular budgeting method is the 50/30/20 rule, which is simple and effective:

- 50% for Needs: This includes all the fixed expenses like housing, utilities, groceries, transportation, insurance, and minimum debt payments.
- 30% for Wants: This category includes discretionary spending, such as entertainment, dining out, vacations, and shopping.
- 20% for Savings and Debt Repayment: This portion goes toward saving for future goals, paying off high-interest debt, or investing in your retirement fund.

This rule is flexible—adjust the percentages based on your specific financial situation. For example, if your rent is significantly high, you may need to allocate more toward needs and less toward wants. The goal is to ensure that you have enough money for your necessities while still making progress toward your financial goals.

4. Identify Areas for Cutting Unnecessary Costs

One of the most important aspects of budgeting is being able to identify areas where you can cut back. Once you've tracked your expenses and categorized them, it's time to analyze where you can make adjustments.

Cutting Back on Discretionary Spending

Discretionary expenses are often the easiest to cut because they are non-essential. For instance, if you dine out frequently, you might consider cooking at home more often, which can save a significant amount of money. Other areas for cutting back may include:

- Streaming Services: If you're subscribed to multiple streaming platforms but rarely use them, consider canceling or downgrading your subscriptions.
- Subscriptions: Cancel any subscription services, magazines, or memberships you're no longer using or don't need.
- Impulse Purchases: Before making a purchase, pause and ask yourself if it's something you truly need or if it's an impulse buy. You can avoid unnecessary purchases by giving yourself a cooling-off period of a day or two.

Reducing Fixed Expenses

While fixed expenses may seem less flexible, there are still opportunities to cut costs:

- Refinance Debt: If you have high-interest debt, consider consolidating or refinancing loans to lower your interest rate. This can help reduce your monthly payments.
- Downsize Housing: If your rent or mortgage is a significant portion of your income, consider downsizing to a more affordable home or apartment.
- Switch Utility Providers: Some utilities, like insurance, phone plans, and internet, offer the potential to reduce costs by switching providers or negotiating for better rates.

Reducing Variable Expenses

Even though these expenses fluctuate, there are plenty of opportunities to save:

- Shop Smarter: Use coupons, shop during sales, or buy in bulk to lower the cost of groceries.

- Energy Savings: Reduce electricity bills by being mindful of turning off lights, unplugging devices, and using energy-efficient appliances.
- Public Transportation: If you drive to work, consider taking public transportation or carpooling to save on fuel and parking costs.

5. Track Your Progress and Make Adjustments

Budgeting is a dynamic process. Once you've set up your budget and started tracking your expenses, review your progress regularly. At the end of each month, check if you've met your savings goals and whether you stuck to your budget. If you find that you overspent in one category, look for areas in the next month where you can cut back to make up for it. Small adjustments here and there will help you stay on track toward your financial goals.

Setting up a budget is a powerful tool that gives you control over your financial future. By tracking your spending, categorizing your expenses, and identifying unnecessary costs, you'll be able to prioritize your needs, cut back on your wants, and allocate more money toward your savings and debt repayment. Building a budget may take some time and effort, but once you've set it up and established good habits, you'll be on your way to financial security and freedom. Remember, budgeting is not about restricting yourself; it's about making conscious decisions that align with your goals and values.

Identifying Financial Goals: Short-term vs. Long-term

When it comes to managing personal finances, one of the most crucial steps is identifying and setting clear financial goals. Financial goals give you a roadmap for managing your money, allowing you to make informed decisions and prioritize your spending. Broadly speaking, financial goals can be categorized into short-term and long-term goals. Understanding the difference between these two categories and how they impact your financial planning is essential for achieving financial stability and independence.

What Are Financial Goals?

Financial goals are specific objectives that you set for yourself to achieve a desired financial outcome. These goals can vary in terms of the amount of time required to achieve them and the level of financial commitment they demand. While some financial goals might be achievable in a few months, others might take years of consistent effort to accomplish. By having clear financial goals, you can focus on what's most important and work toward attaining those objectives over time.

Short-term Financial Goals

Short-term financial goals are those objectives that you aim to achieve within a year or two. These goals typically require less time and money compared to long-term goals, making them more manageable. Short-term goals are the foundation upon which long-term financial success can be built. They allow you to take incremental steps toward larger financial ambitions.

Examples of short-term financial goals include:

- Building an Emergency Fund: Setting aside three to six months' worth of living expenses in a liquid, easily accessible account can provide financial security in case of unexpected events such as medical emergencies or job loss. An emergency fund is a crucial financial cushion and is often a primary goal for many individuals when starting their financial journey.

- Paying Off Credit Card Debt: Credit card debt usually comes with high interest rates, which can accumulate quickly. Paying off high-interest debt in the short term is often a priority, as it prevents financial strain in the future and saves money on interest payments.

- Saving for a Vacation or Large Purchase: Short-term goals can also involve saving for things like vacations, home renovations, or other significant but non-essential purchases. These goals often have a timeline and a set dollar amount, making them easier to track and achieve.

- Setting Up a Budget: One of the first steps in achieving financial success is creating and sticking to a budget. A well-structured budget allows you to allocate funds for essential expenses while also setting aside money for savings and discretionary spending. This goal is critical for developing good financial habits.

The advantage of short-term goals is that they tend to be relatively quick to achieve, providing a sense of accomplishment and motivation to continue working toward more significant financial milestones. Moreover, achieving short-term goals builds discipline and allows you to assess your financial habits, which are vital for long-term success.

Long-term Financial Goals

Long-term financial goals, on the other hand, are those that take more time to achieve—typically three to five years or even decades. These goals often involve more substantial financial commitments and can include life-changing milestones, such as purchasing a home, saving for retirement, or funding a child's education.

Examples of long-term financial goals include:

- Saving for Retirement: One of the most common long-term financial goals is preparing for retirement. This often involves setting up a retirement savings plan, such as a 401(k) or an individual retirement account (IRA), and contributing consistently over the years. The earlier you start, the more time your investments have to grow, compounding over time. The goal is to accumulate enough funds to maintain your desired lifestyle once you stop working.

- Buying a Home: Purchasing a home is often a significant milestone in a person's financial life. Saving for a down payment, securing a mortgage, and budgeting for homeownership expenses like taxes and maintenance are critical aspects of this long-term goal. Homeownership often requires years of saving and planning, especially when accounting for large initial payments and monthly costs.

- Saving for a Child's Education: If you have children, saving for their education can be a long-term financial goal. The cost of college tuition and other educational expenses can add up over the years, and starting a college savings plan early can reduce the burden when the time comes. The use of tax-advantaged accounts like 529 plans is one common method for saving for a child's education.

- Building Wealth and Financial Independence: Many people aim to build long-term wealth and achieve financial independence, meaning they no longer have to rely on earned income to cover their expenses. This goal often involves investing in assets such as stocks, bonds, real estate, or businesses. Over time, the goal is to accumulate enough wealth to achieve a passive income that covers living expenses.

- Paying Off a Mortgage: A mortgage is one of the largest financial commitments many people will take on in their lifetime. Paying off a mortgage early can provide a significant sense of financial freedom, as it removes a large monthly payment and increases overall wealth. This goal may take decades to achieve, depending on the mortgage's terms and the individual's financial situation.

While long-term goals can take many years or even decades to achieve, they are typically more rewarding. The process of working toward these goals requires consistency, discipline, and long-term financial planning. Achieving long-term financial goals is often tied to reaching a state of financial security and freedom, allowing individuals to retire comfortably, send their children to school, or leave a financial legacy for future generations.

How Short-Term and Long-Term Goals Work Together

Short-term and long-term financial goals are not mutually exclusive—they work in tandem to create a comprehensive financial plan. Short-term goals often provide the immediate steps and milestones that help set the stage for achieving long-term goals. For example, you might focus on paying off credit card debt (a short-term goal) to free up money for long-term savings, such as building an emergency fund or investing for retirement.

Similarly, reaching short-term milestones can give you the confidence and financial stability needed to stay on track for your long-term goals. As you build a foundation with short-term achievements, you are better prepared to take on the larger, more complex tasks associated with long-term financial planning.

Setting SMART Goals for Both Short-Term and Long-Term Success

To effectively achieve both short-term and long-term financial goals, it's important to apply the SMART goal framework. SMART stands for:

- Specific: Clearly define the goal. What exactly do you want to accomplish? For example, "I want to save $5,000 for an emergency fund in the next 12 months."

- Measurable: Make sure you can track progress. This could mean tracking savings in a bank account, tracking debt repayment amounts, or setting a specific target for investment growth.

- Achievable: Ensure the goal is realistic based on your current financial situation. A goal should be challenging but not unattainable.

- Relevant: Ensure the goal aligns with your overall financial objectives and life circumstances.

- Time-bound: Set a clear deadline for achieving the goal. This helps you stay focused and motivated.

Whether working toward short-term or long-term financial goals, following the SMART framework can help you stay on track and make measurable progress toward your desired financial outcomes.

Identifying your financial goals is one of the most important steps in securing your financial future. Short-term goals help you build a solid foundation, while long-term goals allow you to achieve major life milestones, such as homeownership, retirement, and financial independence. Both types of goals are interconnected, and achieving them requires careful planning, discipline, and patience.

By defining your goals clearly and applying a strategic approach, you can take control of your financial destiny and work toward the life you've always envisioned. Whether you're saving for a vacation or building wealth for the future, identifying both short-term and long-term goals is the key to financial success.

The Psychology of Money

The way we think about and approach money is shaped by far more than just logic, economics, or financial strategies. It's heavily influenced by our emotions, experiences, and psychological factors. The psychology of money is a complex and multifaceted topic that explores the behaviors, beliefs, and decisions that govern how people handle money, accumulate wealth, and make financial choices. This intricate relationship between psychology and money reveals how human emotions can impact financial decisions and often lead to actions that aren't always in our best interest.

Our Emotional Relationship with Money

Money is not just a medium of exchange; it's a symbol of power, security, freedom, and sometimes even happiness. How we view money often stems from our upbringing, personal experiences, and societal influences. For example, people who grew up in a household where money was scarce might develop a mindset rooted in scarcity, fear, and a strong desire to accumulate wealth for security. On the other hand, those who grew up in a financially stable environment may develop a different perspective on money, often viewing it as something to be enjoyed or used to enrich life experiences rather than as something to fear losing.

Our relationship with money can also be tied to our values and identity. Some people derive their sense of self-worth from their financial success, equating wealth with their personal value. Others may feel shame or guilt around money, possibly due to financial struggles or cultural stigmas. This emotional connection can dictate how we save, spend, or invest money, often leading to choices based on fear, guilt, or pride instead of rational thought.

The Role of Cognitive Biases in Financial Decision-Making

Humans are not always as logical and rational as they think. Cognitive biases—systematic patterns of deviation from rationality—often influence our decision-making processes, especially when it comes to money. These biases shape how we perceive and evaluate financial choices, leading to poor decisions that can derail long-term financial health.

One common cognitive bias is loss aversion, which refers to the tendency to feel the pain of losing something more intensely than the pleasure of gaining something of equal value. This bias often leads people to hold on to losing investments or underperforming assets simply because they don't want to experience the emotional pain of realizing a loss. Similarly, people might avoid taking financial risks, even if those risks offer a higher potential for reward, simply because they fear the possibility of losing what they already have.

Another influential cognitive bias is overconfidence. Many individuals believe they can outsmart the market or predict future outcomes, which leads to overactive trading, unnecessary risks, and poor investment decisions. Overconfidence can also manifest in the form of underestimating the importance of saving for the future or thinking they can easily "make it big" without putting in the necessary effort or time.

The anchoring effect is another bias that can impact financial decisions. This occurs when individuals rely too heavily on the first piece of information they encounter—often an initial price or estimate—even when it's irrelevant. For example, a person might focus on a product's original price and believe that a discount represents an incredible deal, when in reality, the discounted price is still more than what the item is worth. This bias can lead to overspending and poor financial choices.

The Impact of Financial Anxiety

Money-related stress, often referred to as financial anxiety, is a widespread issue that affects many people across different socioeconomic backgrounds. Financial anxiety is the feeling of fear, worry, or stress related to one's financial situation or financial future. People who experience financial anxiety may worry about not having enough money to pay bills, save for retirement, or maintain their desired lifestyle. This anxiety can lead to a cycle of poor decision-making, avoidance, or procrastination when it comes to addressing financial issues.

For some individuals, financial anxiety can result in compulsive spending or even hoarding. People who fear losing their financial stability may engage in excessive saving to an unhealthy degree, leading to a lack of enjoyment in life. On the other hand, individuals with an avoidant approach to money might struggle to address their finances at all, which can exacerbate their financial issues and increase anxiety. Over time, chronic financial anxiety can negatively impact overall well-being and make it more challenging to make clear, rational decisions.

The Influence of Societal and Cultural Factors

Society and culture play an essential role in shaping our attitudes toward money. The values and beliefs surrounding wealth, status, and success are often influenced by cultural norms and social expectations. For instance, in cultures that prioritize material wealth and financial success, individuals may feel pressure to live up to these expectations, leading to a focus on outward appearances and status symbols rather than financial well-being.

In addition to societal pressures, social media plays a significant role in shaping modern perceptions of wealth and success. The constant stream of curated, idealized images of wealthy individuals and luxurious lifestyles can make others feel inadequate or envious, prompting them to make financial decisions that don't align with their true values or long-term goals. The desire to keep up with others can lead to overspending, taking on debt, or engaging in unhealthy financial behaviors.

Money Scripts: Beliefs About Money That Shape Our Lives

Another key concept in the psychology of money is the idea of money scripts. Money scripts are the deep-seated beliefs that individuals hold about money, often formed in childhood or early adulthood. These scripts act as guiding principles and can significantly influence financial behaviors later in life.

Some common money scripts include beliefs such as "money is the root of all evil," "I will never be rich," or "I need to work hard to earn money." These scripts may be conscious or unconscious, but they often dictate how we manage our finances. If someone believes that money is evil, they may avoid accumulating wealth or fail to set financial goals. On the other hand, someone who believes that hard work is the only way to get rich might work excessive hours but fail to achieve financial freedom because they neglect the importance of savings, investing, and wealth-building strategies.

Recognizing and challenging money scripts is a crucial step in understanding the psychology of money and developing healthier financial habits. By examining how our beliefs about money shape our actions, we can begin to make more informed decisions and break free from patterns that hold us back from financial success.

The psychology of money is a multifaceted topic that delves into the way emotions, biases, and beliefs shape our financial decisions. From our emotional attachment to money to the cognitive biases that distort our judgment, understanding the psychological aspects of money can lead to more mindful and effective financial behaviors. By recognizing the impact of societal pressures, financial anxiety, and personal money scripts, individuals can develop healthier relationships with money and achieve greater financial well-being. Ultimately, understanding the psychology of money is not just about managing wealth—it's about making empowered choices that align with our values, goals, and long-term happiness.

Mindset Shifts Needed to Save Money

Saving money is often portrayed as a simple task: spend less than you earn, and the savings will follow. However, for many individuals, saving money can feel like an ongoing struggle. The challenge isn't necessarily in the mechanics of saving but in our mindset and beliefs around money. How we perceive, approach, and engage with money directly impacts our ability to save and build wealth. Therefore, changing our mindset is one of the most crucial steps toward financial success. Let's dive into the key mindset shifts needed to start saving money effectively.

1. Adopting a Long-Term View on Money

One of the first mindset shifts needed to save money is moving away from a short-term perspective and adopting a long-term view. In today's consumer-driven world, we are often conditioned to focus on instant gratification — buying things now and worrying about the future later. However, saving money requires shifting your mindset to prioritize long-term financial goals over immediate desires.

By thinking long-term, we understand that every small decision we make today affects our financial future. It's essential to view saving money not as a one-time goal but as a continual habit that builds over time. Whether you're saving for a down payment on a home, your children's education, or retirement, taking a long-term approach ensures that your money works for you, even when you're not actively thinking about it.

2. Believing in Financial Abundance

Many people live under the belief that money is scarce and hard to come by, often feeling like there's never enough. This mindset leads to feelings of anxiety and the belief that no matter how hard they work, they'll always fall short of financial security. To counter this, it's important to shift your perspective to one of financial abundance.

This doesn't mean that money grows on trees or that we should live without financial discipline, but it does mean understanding that wealth is created through intentional actions, smart decisions, and the right mindset. Abundance encourages the belief that there are plenty of opportunities to make money, grow savings, and achieve financial goals. This shift opens you to new possibilities, helping you adopt healthier habits, explore side hustles, and optimize your earning potential.

3. Shifting from Spending to Saving

A significant shift in mindset for many is the move from thinking of money primarily as something to spend to viewing it as something to save and invest. Our culture often emphasizes spending on things that promise immediate satisfaction — shopping, dining out, and entertainment. However, those instant gratifications often lead to long-term regrets when they prevent us from building a financial safety net.

To foster the habit of saving, it's crucial to change your thinking around the purpose of money. Instead of seeing money as something to use for momentary pleasures, begin to see it as a tool that gives you freedom and security in the future. When you view saving as an essential part of your life, you begin to make smarter spending decisions and find joy in setting aside funds for your future self.

4. Understanding the Power of Small Changes

One common barrier to saving money is the belief that you need to make dramatic lifestyle changes to save effectively. Many people feel that they need to overhaul their entire financial situation before seeing results. The reality is, small changes can make a significant difference over time.

Shifting your mindset to understand the compounding effect of small, consistent savings is key. Cutting out an unnecessary subscription or bringing lunch to work might seem insignificant at first, but when done consistently, these actions add up. By focusing on small, manageable changes, you reduce the overwhelming feeling that saving requires monumental sacrifice. This approach allows you to start saving without feeling deprived or stressed.

5. Seeing Sacrifice as Temporary, Not Permanent

Another critical shift in mindset when it comes to saving money is changing how you perceive sacrifice. Many people associate saving with sacrifice, assuming it means living without enjoyment, always saying no to their desires. While it's true that saving often involves making trade-offs, it's important to view these sacrifices as temporary rather than permanent.

Saving money isn't about denying yourself joy forever; it's about prioritizing your future well-being. The short-term discomfort you might feel by cutting back on some expenses is nothing compared to the long-term freedom and financial security you gain. By reframing sacrifices as temporary and part of a bigger picture, you'll be more motivated to stick to your savings plan and push through any initial discomfort.

6. Focusing on Value, Not Price

Another major mindset shift involves moving away from focusing purely on price and toward considering the value of purchases. Many people make financial decisions based on the price of an item alone, ignoring whether the purchase is truly valuable in the long run. This can result in impulse buying and unnecessary expenditures.

By shifting your focus to value, you make decisions that benefit your life in a more meaningful way. For instance, a higher-priced item might offer greater durability and serve you for many years, which makes it a smarter long-term investment. On the other hand, cheaper, lower-quality options may lead to frequent replacements, costing more in the end. The key here is to ask yourself: Does this purchase contribute to my overall goals, or is it simply an emotional spend?

7. Becoming Comfortable with Delayed Gratification

Delayed gratification is the concept of postponing immediate pleasure for greater rewards in the future. It's one of the most essential mindset shifts needed to save money effectively. In our fast-paced society, we're often urged to buy things immediately. However, the ability to delay gratification allows you to save for bigger goals, such as a home, education, or retirement.

This mindset isn't about never having fun or enjoying life, but about recognizing that some of the most meaningful rewards require patience. Whether it's saving for a vacation or working toward a large financial milestone, learning to enjoy the process of delayed gratification will help you develop better money habits and set you on a path to long-term financial success.

8. Viewing Money as a Tool, Not a Goal

Finally, it's essential to shift your perspective on money itself. Many people view money as the ultimate goal — the thing they're working toward. However, money is merely a tool that allows us to achieve our true goals, such as security, freedom, and happiness. By viewing money as a means to an end, rather than the end itself, you are better able to prioritize your financial decisions in alignment with your core values.

This shift encourages you to think beyond the numbers in your bank account and focus on how your financial choices can support the life you want to lead. It turns the concept of saving into a purposeful action, providing the foundation for a life of financial stability and personal fulfillment.

Saving money is more than just a mechanical task; it's a mindset that drives your financial success. By shifting your perspective on money and focusing on long-term goals, financial abundance, small changes, temporary sacrifices, value, delayed gratification, and viewing money as a tool, you set yourself up for a life of financial stability and security. Remember, the journey toward financial freedom starts with the right mindset — so start cultivating these shifts today, and watch your savings grow!

How to Overcome Emotional Spending Habits

Emotional spending is a pattern where individuals make purchases as a way to cope with their emotions, whether they are feeling stressed, anxious, sad, or even overly joyful. For some, spending becomes a temporary escape or a form of self-reward. However, over time, emotional spending can lead to financial difficulties, creating more stress and making it harder to break the cycle. The good news is, emotional spending can be controlled and eliminated with awareness and intentional strategies.

Here are several steps to help you overcome emotional spending habits and regain control over your finances.

1. Acknowledge the Problem

The first step in overcoming any habit, including emotional spending, is acknowledging that you have a problem. Emotional spending is often a subconscious behavior, so the first thing to do is reflect on your patterns and identify when you're spending due to your emotions. Keep a journal or track your purchases for a month to observe whether there are any triggers or patterns related to your emotional state. For example, you may find that when you're feeling down or bored, you're more likely to make purchases online or impulsively buy something you don't need.

Once you've recognized the problem, it becomes easier to take action to fix it.

2. Identify the Triggers

Understanding what triggers your emotional spending is crucial for stopping it. Emotional spending is typically linked to specific emotions or situations. These triggers could include:

- Stress: Work pressure, family obligations, or personal challenges can trigger a desire to escape through shopping.
- Sadness or Loneliness: Many people shop when they feel isolated, seeking to comfort themselves or fill the emotional void.

- Celebrations or Joy: On the flip side, feelings of elation or celebration might prompt impulsive purchases to reward oneself.
- Boredom: When there's little to do, some people turn to shopping to fill the empty space in their lives.

Once you identify these triggers, you can start working to address them in healthier ways, making it less likely that you'll turn to spending when emotions arise.

3. Find Alternative Coping Mechanisms

After identifying your emotional triggers, the next step is to find healthier ways to cope with these emotions. Emotional spending often acts as a temporary solution to emotional discomfort. Instead of turning to shopping, try adopting alternative strategies that are emotionally fulfilling without the financial cost. Here are a few alternatives to emotional spending:

- Exercise: Physical activity is a great way to relieve stress and improve mood. Even a short walk or a session of yoga can help clear your mind and lower your stress levels.
- Meditation and Mindfulness: Both of these practices help you become more aware of your emotions in the present moment, helping you resist the urge to make an impulse purchase. Meditation allows you to slow down and be more deliberate in your decision-making.
- Creative Hobbies: Try redirecting your energy into creative hobbies like painting, journaling, cooking, or knitting. These activities can be therapeutic and provide a sense of accomplishment without the need to spend money.
- Talking to a Friend or Therapist: Sometimes, the best way to deal with emotions is to talk them through. Call a friend, family member,

or a therapist to process what you're feeling before reaching for your wallet.

4. Create a Budget

One of the most effective ways to control emotional spending is by setting up a strict budget. When you know exactly where your money should go each month, it becomes easier to make more mindful choices about your spending. Start by:

- Tracking Your Income and Expenses: Write down all of your sources of income and all your regular monthly expenses. This helps you visualize where your money is going.
- Setting Spending Limits: Once you've established a baseline for your expenses, allocate a set amount for discretionary spending (such as shopping, dining out, or entertainment). Make sure this amount is realistic, and don't allow yourself to exceed it.
- Setting Financial Goals: Create specific savings or debt-reduction goals. Having these goals in mind helps you stay focused on the long-term picture and discourages impulsive purchases.

By sticking to a budget, you make it easier to evaluate whether a purchase is truly necessary or if it's an emotional reaction. A budget empowers you to make intentional decisions instead of mindless spending.

5. Avoid Temptations and Remove Triggers

One way to curb emotional spending is to limit your exposure to situations and places that trigger it. If you find that online shopping is your primary downfall, consider taking steps such as:

- Unsubscribing from Promotional Emails: These emails often encourage impulse buying. If you don't see a constant stream of sales and discounts, you might be less likely to make purchases based on emotional triggers.

- Removing Shopping Apps: Delete shopping apps from your phone to avoid the temptation to browse when you're bored, stressed, or upset.

- Avoiding Malls and Stores: If you're someone who tends to shop when you're out and about, avoid stores or shopping malls that tempt you to buy things on a whim. If you don't see it, you won't buy it.

- Implement a 24-Hour Rule: When you feel the urge to buy something on impulse, set a rule to wait for at least 24 hours before making the purchase. Often, after this cooling-off period, you'll realize you don't need or want the item after all.

By removing or limiting exposure to your emotional triggers, you make it easier to resist the urge to spend impulsively.

6. Practice Gratitude and Mindfulness

Practicing gratitude and mindfulness on a daily basis can have a profound impact on your emotional health and your spending habits. Mindfulness encourages you to live in the present moment, reducing stress and anxiety. When you practice mindfulness, you're more aware of your feelings and can pause before making purchases based on emotional reactions.

Gratitude, on the other hand, helps you shift your focus from what you don't have to what you do have. Instead of looking for external purchases to bring you happiness, practicing gratitude helps you appreciate the things you already own and the life you already have.

You can incorporate gratitude into your life by keeping a gratitude journal, where you write down three things you're thankful for each day. This helps you stay grounded and less prone to seeking temporary fixes through spending.

7. Seek Professional Help If Necessary

In some cases, emotional spending may be linked to deeper emotional or psychological issues, such as depression, anxiety, or compulsive behavior. If you find it extremely difficult to stop emotional spending, despite your best efforts, it may be helpful to consult a therapist or financial counselor. These professionals can help you identify the root causes of your behavior and work with you to develop healthier coping mechanisms.

Emotional spending can take a toll on your finances, relationships, and overall well-being, but it's not an insurmountable issue. By acknowledging the problem, understanding your triggers, and developing healthier ways to cope with emotions, you can regain control over your spending habits. With a combination of self-awareness, planning, and commitment to your financial goals, emotional spending can become a thing of the past. Ultimately, overcoming emotional spending is about fostering a sense of peace and fulfillment that doesn't rely on material possessions.

The Importance of Self-Discipline in Managing Money

Self-discipline is one of the most crucial components in effectively managing money and achieving financial success. Whether you are a student, a young professional, or someone planning for retirement, the ability to exercise self-control over your finances is key to maintaining financial health and stability. While many people believe that financial success is achieved through making a large amount of money, it is often how you manage and control that money that truly determines your financial well-being. Let's explore why self-discipline plays such a vital role in managing money, and how adopting this trait can change your financial future for the better.

1. Understanding the Need for Self-Discipline in Financial Management

Self-discipline refers to the ability to control one's emotions, behaviors, and actions in the face of external demands, to achieve a greater goal or objective. In financial terms, self-discipline is the conscious effort to manage your spending, savings, and investment habits in a way that aligns with your long-term financial goals.

Without self-discipline, even individuals with high incomes can fall into financial trouble. Overspending, impulsive purchases, and a lack of budgeting can prevent individuals from saving or investing for the future. Therefore, a solid sense of discipline enables individuals to remain committed to their financial goals, avoid unnecessary purchases, and work toward building a secure future.

2. Creating and Sticking to a Budget

One of the most fundamental aspects of managing money is budgeting. A budget is essentially a plan that helps individuals track their income and allocate it toward different expenses and savings. Without a budget, it's easy to spend beyond your means and fall into debt.

Self-discipline is what ensures you stick to your budget, even when it's tempting to make impulse purchases. It's the ability to say "no" to unnecessary expenses, and the strength to adhere to limits you've set for yourself. By sticking to a well-defined budget, you ensure that your essential needs—like housing, transportation, and food—are met while also allocating money for savings and investments. Moreover, disciplined budgeting prevents you from living paycheck to paycheck, which provides peace of mind and reduces stress.

3. Building Healthy Financial Habits

Self-discipline plays a significant role in the development of healthy financial habits. Whether it's regularly setting aside money for an emergency fund, making consistent contributions to retirement savings, or tracking expenses, good financial habits help individuals to manage money effectively.

For example, contributing a fixed percentage of your income to your savings each month can become a regular habit if you approach it with self-discipline. This habit may seem small at first, but over time, it will accumulate into a substantial financial cushion that can help you weather unexpected expenses or retirement.

Discipline also extends to your spending habits. For instance, instead of splurging on a luxury item every time you feel the urge, individuals with strong financial discipline know how to distinguish between wants and needs. They're able to delay gratification, which leads to healthier financial decisions in the long term.

4. Avoiding Impulse Spending

Impulse spending is a major obstacle that prevents many people from managing their money effectively. It's easy to get caught up in the moment and purchase something you don't really need, whether it's an item on sale, a new gadget, or an impulse online purchase.

Self-discipline helps you recognize these temptations and resist them. Individuals who practice financial discipline often create strategies to avoid the pitfalls of impulse spending, such as creating shopping lists, setting spending limits, or leaving credit cards at home while running errands. By planning ahead and sticking to your plans, you prevent yourself from making spur-of-the-moment purchases that can derail your financial goals.

5. Saving and Investing for the Future

The future is uncertain, and that's why building savings and making investments for long-term financial security is so important. However, saving and investing require a long-term view and patience. It is easy to forgo saving for the future in favor of enjoying instant pleasures today, but this can be detrimental to your financial health.

Self-discipline is what allows you to consistently save and invest for the future. Whether it's making automatic transfers to a retirement account or making regular contributions to an emergency fund, disciplined financial behaviors ensure that you're building a financial safety net for later in life. Furthermore, financial self-discipline allows you to stick to a long-term investment strategy, resist panic during market fluctuations, and avoid making rash financial decisions.

6. Eliminating Debt

Debt is one of the leading causes of financial stress. While debt can sometimes be necessary, especially for large purchases like a home or education, it can quickly spiral out of control if not managed responsibly.

Self-discipline is essential for debt management. If you're paying down high-interest credit card debt, for example, self-discipline means resisting the urge to add new purchases to the balance, making consistent payments toward your debt, and finding ways to limit your reliance on credit. Those who develop strong financial discipline make it a priority to eliminate debt as quickly as possible, leading to a debt-free life where financial freedom is achievable.

7. Building Financial Confidence

When you maintain self-discipline in managing your money, you gradually build confidence in your financial decisions. Consistently sticking to a budget, saving for the future, and avoiding impulsive purchases can give you a sense of control over your financial life. This sense of confidence leads to better financial decision-making and provides a stronger foundation for pursuing financial goals.

Self-discipline doesn't only create a secure financial future, but it can also improve your mental and emotional well-being. The less you worry about money, the more confident and empowered you feel about your financial future.

8. Facing Financial Setbacks with Resilience

Even with the best financial plans in place, life can throw unexpected financial challenges your way. Whether it's an emergency medical expense, a job loss, or a sudden dip in your investments, setbacks are part of life.

However, individuals with self-discipline are more likely to handle financial setbacks with resilience. Because they have a habit of saving, living below their means, and making sound financial choices, they are better prepared to weather these challenges. Instead of giving in to stress or panic, those with self-discipline know that they can take charge of their financial situation, adjust their plan, and get back on track.

Self-discipline is the foundation of good financial management. Without it, it's all too easy to fall into the traps of overspending, accumulating debt, and failing to save for the future. By practicing financial self-discipline, you can stick to a budget, build healthy financial habits, save and invest for the future, and ultimately achieve your financial goals. It's a long-term commitment that requires patience, consistency, and resilience, but the rewards of financial freedom and security are well worth the effort. By developing self-discipline, you empower yourself to take control of your financial future and live the life you deserve.

Practical Tips for Saving Money Daily

Saving money can often feel like an overwhelming task, especially in today's world where costs seem to rise constantly. However, the key to financial stability is not necessarily making large cuts to your spending, but making small, consistent changes every day that add up over time. In this chapter, we'll explore practical tips you can start implementing right now to save money on a daily basis, and how those small savings can lead to big results in the long run.

1. Track Your Spending

Before making any changes to your budget, it's important to understand where your money is going. By tracking your spending, you can identify areas where you may be overspending or making unnecessary purchases. Start by keeping a daily log of everything you buy, no matter how small. Use a budgeting app or simply keep a notebook where you jot down your expenses. At the end of the week or month, review your spending habits and highlight areas where you can cut back. This step is essential for understanding the impact of your daily habits on your overall financial situation.

2. Eliminate Small, Repetitive Purchases

Many of us don't think twice about spending small amounts of money on daily purchases, such as coffee, snacks, or convenience foods. However, these small expenses add up quickly and can be a drain on your savings. Try bringing your own coffee or snacks from home, or consider meal prepping for the week to reduce the need for expensive takeout. Cutting out these small, unnecessary purchases may seem insignificant, but over time, the savings can be substantial. Consider setting a budget for these items each week and stick to it.

3. Set Up Automatic Savings

One of the most effective ways to save money consistently is by automating the process. Set up an automatic transfer from your checking account to your savings account every time you get paid. This ensures that a portion of your income goes straight into savings before you have a chance to spend it. Even a small amount, such as 20 or 50 per paycheck, can add up over time and provide a financial cushion in case of emergencies. Treat your savings like a bill you must pay, and you'll be less likely to spend that money impulsively.

4. Pack Your Lunch

Eating out for lunch every day is one of the easiest ways to waste money. Even if you're only spending $5 to $10 a day on lunch, that adds up to $25 to $50 per week, or $100 to $200 a month. Instead, consider packing your lunch from home. Not only will this save you money, but you'll also have more control over the quality and nutritional value of the food you're eating. Prepare meals in advance, and use leftovers from dinner to create easy-to-grab lunches for the next day.

5. Limit Impulse Purchases

Impulse buying is one of the biggest obstacles to saving money. From online shopping to spontaneous trips to the store, these unplanned purchases can quickly eat into your savings. One effective way to limit impulse purchases is by creating a shopping list and sticking to it. Whether you're buying groceries or clothing, always shop with a list in hand, and avoid browsing through aisles or websites without a specific purpose. Another helpful strategy is the "24-hour rule." If you're tempted to buy something on a whim, give yourself 24 hours to think about it. By the time the day is up, you may find that you no longer feel the urge to buy it.

6. Reduce Energy Consumption

Small changes in your daily routine can lead to significant savings on your utility bills. Turn off lights when they're not in use, unplug electronics that aren't being used, and switch to energy-efficient light bulbs. Another great way to save on energy costs is by adjusting your thermostat. In the winter, lowering the temperature by a few degrees can save a noticeable amount on heating costs. Similarly, in the summer, raise the thermostat a few degrees to reduce cooling costs. These energy-saving habits will not only help you save money, but they also contribute to a greener planet.

7. Use Public Transportation or Carpool

Transportation is one of the largest expenses in most people's budgets. Instead of driving every day, consider using public transportation or carpooling with coworkers or friends. If you live in a city with a reliable public transit system, this can save you a significant amount of money on gas, parking, and car maintenance. Even if public transit isn't an option, carpooling can reduce your transportation costs and help you share the expense with others.

8. Cancel Unused Subscriptions

In today's world, subscription services have become a norm, whether it's for streaming platforms, magazines, or gym memberships. While these services can be convenient, many of us forget to cancel subscriptions we no longer use. Take an inventory of all the subscriptions you're currently paying for and evaluate whether you really need them. Do you still watch that streaming service? Are you using that gym membership? If not, cancel the subscriptions and redirect that money to your savings account.

9. Buy in Bulk

For items you use regularly, buying in bulk can save you a significant amount of money in the long run. This applies to everything from groceries to household supplies like toilet paper and cleaning products. By purchasing in bulk, you're often paying less per unit and reducing the frequency of your shopping trips. Just make sure to only buy items that you know you'll use before they expire, as buying in bulk won't save you money if the products go to waste.

10. Take Advantage of Coupons and Discounts

It may seem time-consuming, but using coupons and taking advantage of discounts is an easy way to save money. Whether it's a percentage off your grocery bill or a special promotion for clothing, every little bit helps. Make it a habit to check for coupons or promo codes before making any purchase, both online and in-store. Many stores also offer loyalty programs or apps that provide special discounts to members, so be sure to sign up for those when available.

Saving money doesn't require drastic changes to your lifestyle or income. By implementing just a few of these daily money-saving tips, you can make a big impact on your finances over time. Start small, be consistent, and remember that every penny saved is a step toward building a more secure financial future. With patience and discipline, you can achieve your financial goals and enjoy the peace of mind that comes with a healthy savings account.

Small Daily Changes That Add Up Over Time

Saving money is often viewed as a challenging task, with many individuals believing that in order to make any significant progress, they must make large financial sacrifices or dramatic changes in their lifestyle. However, the truth is that small, consistent adjustments in daily spending habits can have a substantial impact on your overall savings over time. By focusing on small daily changes, you can build better financial habits, increase your savings, and create a stable financial foundation without feeling deprived. Here are some small daily changes that can make a big difference in the long run.

1. Bring Your Own Coffee and Snacks

A daily expense that many people overlook is buying coffee or snacks on the go. It's convenient, but it adds up. If you're spending $4 on a cup of coffee every morning, that's $20 a week, which equals $1,040 per year. Instead, try making coffee at home or preparing your own snacks to take to work. The upfront cost of a coffee maker or a thermos might seem high, but it will pay for itself in a matter of weeks.

Additionally, buying ingredients to prepare homemade snacks rather than purchasing pre-packaged ones can save you even more money. Over time, these small adjustments can lead to significant savings.

2. Cook More at Home

Eating out frequently is another area where money can slip through your fingers. While the occasional meal at a restaurant is fine, regularly dining out can drain your finances without you even realizing it. A meal for two at a mid-range restaurant can easily cost upwards of $50, whereas cooking at home can cost a fraction of that. Even preparing simple meals, like pasta, salads, or soups, can save you hundreds of dollars a month.

Additionally, cooking at home allows you to control portion sizes and ingredients, helping you maintain a healthier lifestyle and further reduce your food costs. Over time, these savings can be significant and contribute to a healthy savings habit.

3. Buy Generic Brands

Many people automatically reach for name-brand products, but often, generic or store brands are just as good, if not better, at a fraction of the price. This applies to everything from groceries to household cleaning products. Over time, switching to generic brands can save you hundreds of dollars annually, which you can redirect toward your savings.

4. Use Cashback and Reward Programs

Taking advantage of cashback offers and reward programs is another small way to save money. Many credit cards offer cashback for every purchase, and some retailers provide loyalty programs that reward you with discounts or points toward future purchases. While it's important not to overspend just to get rewards, using these programs wisely can help you save money over time.

5. Buy Used or Refurbished Items

Instead of always purchasing brand-new items, consider buying used or refurbished products. Many items, such as electronics, furniture, and clothing, can be found in excellent condition at a fraction of the cost. Shopping at thrift stores, second-hand shops, or online marketplaces can help you find high-quality items without paying full price.

Small Changes, Big Results

Incorporating small daily changes into your life can have a profound impact on your savings over time. These changes may not feel like much in the short term, but when compounded over weeks, months, and years, they can add up to significant financial improvements. The key is consistency. By tracking your spending, being mindful of your habits, and making small adjustments, you can build a strong savings habit that sets you up for long-term financial success. Every small step you take today will bring you closer to a brighter, more financially secure future.

Using Coupons and Cashback Apps for Saving Money

In today's fast-paced, consumer-driven society, saving money has become a priority for many. With rising costs of living and fluctuating income, people are constantly looking for effective ways to stretch their dollars further. Fortunately, with the advent of digital technology, we now have access to a range of tools that can make saving money both easy and rewarding. Among these tools, coupons and cashback apps have gained immense popularity for their ability to offer significant savings on everyday purchases. In this article, we will explore how to maximize savings by using coupons and cashback apps effectively.

The Power of Coupons

Coupons have been around for decades, and they've certainly evolved over time. Initially, coupons were physical pieces of paper cut out from newspapers or mailers, offering discounts on products at your local store. Today, however, digital coupons are everywhere. From large retail chains to small online shops, businesses are using coupon codes as a marketing strategy to attract customers.

Using coupons is an excellent way to save money on both essential and luxury items. The key to effectively using coupons is being strategic and organized. Here are some useful tips to maximize your savings with coupons:

1. Subscribe to Newsletter Offers: Many stores and brands offer a discount when you sign up for their newsletter. This can range from a 10% off coupon to free shipping on your next purchase. Make sure to check your inbox regularly for special deals or time-limited offers.

2. Use Coupon Websites and Apps: Websites like RetailMeNot, Honey, and Coupons.com offer hundreds of free digital coupons. All you need to do is browse the site for your favorite store, and it will display available discounts and promo codes. Some apps even allow you to apply the coupons directly while checking out online.

3. Stack Coupons: Some retailers allow customers to stack multiple coupons on a single purchase. For example, you may be able to use one coupon for a percentage off the entire purchase and another one for free shipping. Be sure to check store policies to see if they allow this and always take advantage of it if they do.

4. Check for Store Loyalty Programs: Many stores have loyalty programs that give you access to exclusive coupons and discounts. Signing up for these programs often comes with additional perks, such as birthday discounts or early access to sales events.

5. Couponing for Big Purchases: If you're planning to make a significant purchase, such as furniture, electronics, or a major household item, take time to search for coupons or deals in advance. Retailers often have seasonal sales, special promotions, or clearance events where you can find valuable coupon codes.

By incorporating coupons into your shopping habits, you can lower the overall cost of many products you buy regularly, making your dollar go much further.

The Rise of Cashback Apps

Cashback apps have emerged as an incredibly popular way for consumers to save money while shopping. These apps allow users to earn a percentage of their purchases back in the form of cash, which can be redeemed for direct deposit, gift cards, or PayPal transfers. Cashback apps take the concept of a discount one step further by allowing you to receive a portion of the money you spend back.

Here are some of the most popular cashback apps that can help you earn money while shopping:

1. Rakuten (formerly Ebates): Rakuten is one of the most widely known cashback apps, offering cashback on both online and in-store purchases. By signing up for a free account, you can earn up to 40% cashback on eligible purchases made at major retailers, including

Amazon, Walmart, and Macy's. Rakuten also offers special deals where you can earn extra cashback for specific products or categories.

2. Ibotta: Ibotta is another popular cashback app that works with a wide range of retailers. Whether you're shopping for groceries, clothing, or electronics, Ibotta allows you to earn cashback by simply scanning the receipts from your purchases. The app also has a mobile shopping feature that lets you earn cashback directly from in-app purchases.

3. Dosh: Dosh is a straightforward app that offers cashback on purchases made at participating retailers. It connects with your debit or credit card, so you don't need to scan receipts or clip coupons. Every time you make an eligible purchase, Dosh automatically adds cashback to your account.

4. TopCashback: TopCashback works similarly to Rakuten, offering competitive cashback deals at thousands of online stores. The app also allows you to earn cashback by shopping through its website or browser extension. It is known for offering some of the highest cashback rates available, making it a great choice for savvy shoppers.

5. Swagbucks: Swagbucks is a popular rewards platform where users can earn points (called SB) for performing everyday tasks, such as shopping online, taking surveys, or watching videos. These points can be redeemed for cashback, gift cards, or PayPal payments. Swagbucks often partners with major retailers, providing users with cashback and bonus opportunities for shopping.

Tips for Maximizing Cashback Savings

While using cashback apps can be rewarding, there are ways to enhance your savings and get the most out of these tools:

1. Combine Cashback and Coupons: Many retailers allow you to use both cashback offers and coupon codes simultaneously. By stacking these savings, you can effectively reduce your overall costs even further.

2. Check for Bonus Opportunities: Many cashback apps offer bonus opportunities for specific products, categories, or even shopping at certain retailers. Stay on top of these promotions, as they can provide an additional boost to your cashback earnings.

3. Use Cashback for Everyday Expenses: The more you use cashback apps for your daily purchases, the more money you will save over time. Consider using cashback apps for groceries, household items, and even gas to accumulate cashback rewards that add up quickly.

4. Set Reminders for Expiring Offers: Cashback offers typically come with expiration dates, so it's important to stay organized. Set reminders on your phone or calendar for offers that are about to expire to ensure you don't miss out on potential savings.

5. Be Strategic with In-Store Shopping: Some cashback apps allow you to earn money when you shop in physical stores. By linking your payment cards to your cashback app, you can automatically earn cashback when making in-store purchases at participating retailers.

The combination of coupons and cashback apps has become a powerful way to save money in today's consumer-driven world. By incorporating these tools into your shopping routine, you can take advantage of valuable discounts and earn cashback on many of the things you buy regularly. With the ability to stack savings and find exclusive deals, these digital resources empower you to be a more savvy shopper while building a more rewarding financial future.

Whether you're trying to save money on groceries, fashion, or entertainment, using coupons and cashback apps will ensure that you're always getting the best deal. With just a little planning, you can turn your regular shopping habits into significant savings that can be put toward other goals, such as paying off debt, saving for a vacation, or building your emergency fund. So, start exploring these money-saving tools today, and enjoy the rewards of becoming a smarter, more strategic shopper.

Energy-Saving Hacks to Lower Utility Bills and Save Money

In today's world, where energy consumption is rising and utility bills are steadily increasing, finding ways to reduce energy usage has become essential for both environmental reasons and for our wallets. Lowering your utility bills doesn't require a major overhaul of your lifestyle, but implementing simple yet effective energy-saving hacks can make a significant difference. Whether it's managing your heating and cooling costs, reducing electricity consumption, or finding smarter ways to use water, the following energy-saving hacks will help you lower your utility bills and save money in the long term.

1. Upgrade to Energy-Efficient Appliances

One of the most impactful steps you can take to reduce energy consumption is to replace old, inefficient appliances with energy-efficient models. Modern appliances, such as refrigerators, washing machines, and dishwashers, are designed to use far less energy while providing the same level of performance. Look for appliances that have the ENERGY STAR label, as these are certified to meet energy efficiency guidelines set by the U.S. Environmental Protection Agency (EPA). Although the upfront cost of purchasing energy-efficient appliances may be higher, the savings on your utility bills over time will more than make up for it.

2. Unplug Devices When Not In Use

It's easy to forget, but many electronic devices continue to draw power even when they are turned off. This is known as "phantom" or "standby" power consumption, and it can account for up to 10% of your household energy usage. Appliances like televisions, computers, microwaves, and chargers draw power when plugged in but not in use. To combat this, make a habit of unplugging devices when you're not using them, or invest in a power strip to easily disconnect multiple devices at once.

3. Use Smart Thermostats

Heating and cooling can account for a large portion of your energy bill. A smart thermostat is a game-changer when it comes to reducing these costs. These thermostats learn your preferences and adjust the temperature based on your routine, ensuring that your home is always at the perfect temperature without wasting energy. For example, you can program the thermostat to lower the temperature during the night or when you're away at work. Some smart thermostats can even be controlled remotely via smartphone apps, allowing you to adjust the temperature from anywhere. Over time, you can save a significant amount by optimizing your heating and cooling system.

4. Seal Gaps and Insulate Your Home

Heat loss through doors, windows, and attics can drastically increase your heating and cooling costs. To prevent this, seal any gaps or cracks around windows and doors with weather stripping or caulk. Make sure your windows and doors are properly sealed, and consider adding draft stoppers to keep the warm or cool air inside. Additionally, ensuring that your home is adequately insulated is one of the most effective ways to save energy. Insulation helps to keep the temperature in your home stable, reducing the amount of energy needed for heating and cooling. Pay special attention to areas like the attic and basement, as these are often the primary sources of heat loss.

5. Switch to LED Bulbs

Lighting is another major contributor to electricity costs. Traditional incandescent light bulbs use a lot of energy and have a shorter lifespan compared to newer technologies. By switching to LED bulbs, you can reduce your lighting energy consumption by up to 75%. LED bulbs also last much longer than incandescent bulbs, so you'll save money on replacements as well. Another advantage is that LED lights produce less heat, which means less load on your air conditioning in the summer.

6. Use Energy-Efficient Heating and Cooling Systems

If your heating or cooling system is outdated, it might be time to consider upgrading to a more energy-efficient model. Modern heating and cooling systems, such as heat pumps or high-efficiency furnaces, can significantly reduce your utility bills by using less energy to maintain a comfortable temperature. Additionally, regular maintenance, such as cleaning filters and ensuring proper airflow, can keep your system running efficiently. Scheduling professional maintenance at least once a year can prevent issues that might cause your system to work harder than necessary.

7. Take Shorter Showers and Install Low-Flow Fixtures

Water heating is another hidden cost on your utility bill. Taking long, hot showers and using hot water for laundry can add up quickly. One way to save energy is by shortening your showers, which can save gallons of water and reduce the amount of energy used to heat the water. Additionally, consider installing low-flow showerheads, faucets, and toilets. These fixtures are designed to use less water without compromising performance. By reducing your water usage, you'll not only save on your water bill, but you'll also lower the energy required to heat that water.

8. Use Natural Light

Whenever possible, take advantage of natural light during the day. Open your curtains and blinds to allow sunlight into your home, which can help reduce your need for artificial lighting. This is especially beneficial in the mornings and afternoons when sunlight is abundant. In addition to saving on electricity, natural light has the added benefit of creating a pleasant, vibrant atmosphere in your home. For rooms that need a little more light during the day, consider placing mirrors to reflect natural light deeper into the space.

9. Adjust Your Water Heater Temperature

Your water heater can be another major source of energy consumption.

If the thermostat on your water heater is set too high, it will require more energy to keep the water hot. By adjusting the temperature to 120°F, you can reduce your energy usage by 6-10% without sacrificing comfort. Also, consider insulating your water heater and pipes to help maintain the temperature of the water for longer periods, reducing the need for the heater to kick on as often.

10. Optimize Laundry Practices

Laundry may seem like a small item on your list of energy expenses, but over time, it can add up. Consider washing your clothes in cold water rather than hot to save on energy. Cold water is often sufficient for most loads, and it reduces the strain on your water heater. Also, avoid over-drying clothes in the dryer. Instead, try air-drying clothes when possible, or if you use the dryer, opt for a moisture-sensor feature that stops the dryer when clothes are dry. Additionally, run full loads of laundry to make the most of each cycle.

11. Consider Solar Panels

For a longer-term investment, consider installing solar panels on your roof. Solar energy allows you to harness the power of the sun to generate electricity, which can drastically reduce your utility bills. While the initial cost of installing solar panels can be high, tax incentives and rebates may help lower the cost, and the savings on your utility bills over time can make it a worthwhile investment. In some areas, you may even be able to sell back excess energy to the grid, earning you additional savings.

Reducing your utility bills and saving money on energy is not as difficult as it may seem. By making a few small changes in your daily routine, such as upgrading to energy-efficient appliances, using smart thermostats, or optimizing your heating and cooling system, you can see significant savings over time. Incorporating energy-efficient practices into your lifestyle benefits not only your wallet but also the environment, as it reduces your overall energy consumption. With these simple energy-saving hacks, you can start lowering your utility bills and enjoy a more sustainable and cost-effective way of living.

Building A Savings Fund

Creating a savings fund is one of the foundational elements of financial well-being. Whether you're saving for a rainy day, an emergency, or a specific financial goal, having a robust savings fund in place can provide peace of mind and ensure that you're better prepared for life's unexpected twists and turns. This chapter will guide you through the process of building and managing a savings fund effectively.

Why You Need a Savings Fund

Life is unpredictable. From sudden medical emergencies to car repairs, unexpected expenses can arise at any time. Without a savings fund, you may find yourself relying on credit cards or loans, which can lead to debt and financial strain. A dedicated savings fund acts as a safety net, helping you avoid financial stress when you need it the most.

Additionally, a savings fund enables you to pursue important life goals, like buying a home, traveling, or funding your children's education. By saving consistently and intentionally, you ensure that you're in control of your financial future.

How Much Should You Save?

One of the most common questions when it comes to savings is: How much should I save? While there is no one-size-fits-all answer, many financial experts recommend saving at least 20% of your monthly income. However, the specific amount will depend on your personal financial goals and obligations.

For emergency savings, aim for at least three to six months' worth of living expenses. This amount will ensure that you're covered in case of job loss, unexpected medical bills, or other emergencies. If you're saving for specific goals, such as a vacation or down payment on a house, set a target amount based on the timeline you have in mind.

Tips for Building Your Savings Fund

1. Set Clear Goals:
Before you begin, clearly define the purpose of your savings fund. Are you saving for emergencies, a big purchase, or long-term wealth accumulation? Setting specific, measurable goals will help you stay motivated and focused.

2. Automate Your Savings:
One of the easiest ways to save is by setting up automatic transfers from your checking account to your savings account. By automating your savings, you ensure that the money is put aside before you have the chance to spend it. Treat your savings like a non-negotiable expense, similar to rent or utilities.

3. Start Small, but Start Now:
If you don't have much to put aside at the moment, don't be

discouraged. Even small contributions can add up over time. The key is to start now. Consistency is more important than the size of the contribution. Over time, your savings will grow, and you'll be able to increase your contributions as your financial situation improves.

4. Cut Unnecessary Expenses:
Take a close look at your budget to identify areas where you can cut back. Do you have subscriptions you no longer use? Are you spending too much on dining out or entertainment? Redirect those savings into your savings fund. Small changes can make a big difference.

5. Consider a High-Interest Savings Account:
Look for a savings account that offers a competitive interest rate. While interest rates have been low in recent years, many online banks still offer higher rates than traditional brick-and-mortar institutions. This can help your savings grow faster over time.

6. Build an Emergency Fund First:
While saving for other goals is important, the first priority should always be building an emergency fund. This fund will serve as your financial cushion in case of unexpected events, reducing the need to rely on credit cards or loans when life happens.

7. Track Your Progress:
Regularly check your savings progress to stay motivated. Seeing the growth of your savings can give you a sense of accomplishment and encourage you to keep going. Many banking apps and financial management tools allow you to track your savings goals and see how close you are to reaching them.

Overcoming Challenges in Building a Savings Fund

Building a savings fund is not without its challenges. Life can throw unexpected expenses your way, and sometimes it may feel difficult to stay on track with your savings goals. Here are a few strategies to help you overcome common challenges:

1. Stay Disciplined:
   It's easy to dip into your savings fund for non-emergency expenses, but remember that your savings are there for a reason. Discipline is key to building a strong savings foundation. If you need to, set a specific savings target for each month and resist the temptation to spend it on impulse purchases.

2. Create a Budget:
   If you're struggling to save, it might be helpful to revisit your budget. Create a clear breakdown of your monthly income, expenses, and savings goals. By seeing where your money is going, you may be able to identify areas where you can cut back and allocate more toward your savings fund.

3. Don't Get Discouraged:
   There may be times when you feel like you're not making enough progress. If you can only save a small amount each month, that's okay. Keep going, and remember that building a savings fund takes time. Every little bit adds up, and consistency is the key to long-term success.

4. Review Your Goals:
   Life circumstances change, and your savings goals may shift as well. If you find that your priorities have changed, take a moment to reassess your goals and make adjustments as needed. The important thing is to stay flexible and align your savings plan with your current needs.

Building a savings fund is one of the most important financial steps you can take to secure your future. By setting clear goals, staying disciplined, and automating your savings, you can create a strong financial foundation that will serve you well in times of need and help you achieve your long-term financial dreams. Whether you're saving for an emergency fund, a large purchase, or retirement, taking the time to build a savings fund is an investment in your future financial freedom.

Setting Up an Emergency Savings Fund: A Crucial Step Towards Financial Stability

An emergency savings fund is an essential aspect of financial planning that can provide peace of mind in times of unexpected expenses. Life is unpredictable, and having a financial cushion can make a significant difference when faced with a job loss, medical emergency, car repair, or any other unforeseen costs. In this article, we'll explore why setting up an emergency savings fund is important, how much you should aim to save, and practical steps to build this safety net.

Why You Need an Emergency Savings Fund

1. Unexpected Expenses: Emergencies happen at the most inconvenient times. Without an emergency fund, these unexpected costs can lead to financial hardship, or worse, debt. According to surveys, many Americans are unprepared for financial shocks. Having a dedicated emergency savings account helps prevent you from having to rely on credit cards or loans when things go wrong.

2. Peace of Mind: Knowing that you have funds set aside for emergencies can reduce stress. Rather than feeling anxious about

unexpected expenses, you can approach the situation calmly and confidently, knowing you're prepared for whatever comes your way.

3. Avoiding Debt: One of the biggest reasons people go into debt is because of unexpected expenses. An emergency savings fund can help you avoid using credit cards or loans to cover emergencies. This way, you won't be left with high-interest debt that can linger for months or even years.

4. Financial Independence: The peace of mind that comes from having an emergency savings fund also contributes to financial independence. It provides a buffer that allows you to make choices without fear of financial ruin, such as changing jobs, moving, or taking time off from work.

How Much Should You Save?

Determining how much to save for emergencies can be a tricky question, as everyone's financial situation and needs are different. The general rule of thumb is to save between three to six months' worth of living expenses. This is enough to cover essential expenses in the event of a job loss or other significant life changes.

To calculate how much you need, consider the following:

1. Monthly Expenses: Review your monthly expenses, including rent or mortgage payments, utilities, groceries, transportation, insurance, and debt payments. Add up the total amount you spend each month to get a clear picture of your financial obligations.

2. Your Lifestyle: If you have dependents or live in an area with a

high cost of living, you may need to save more. For example, a family with children or a high-cost city like New York may require a larger emergency fund than someone living alone in a small town.

3. Job Stability: If your job is unstable or you work in a freelance capacity, it's recommended that you save closer to six months of living expenses. If you have a stable, salaried job, three months of savings might be sufficient.

How to Set Up an Emergency Savings Fund

Setting up an emergency savings fund doesn't need to be difficult, but it does require discipline and commitment. Here's a step-by-step guide to help you build your emergency fund:

1. Set a Goal: Start by setting a realistic goal for your emergency savings fund. For example, if your monthly expenses are $2,000, you may aim for a fund of $6,000 to cover three months of expenses. Setting this goal will give you something tangible to work toward.

2. Open a Separate Savings Account: To ensure that your emergency savings is used for emergencies and not for everyday spending, open a separate savings account. Look for an account that offers easy access to your funds but isn't so easily accessible that you're tempted to dip into it for non-emergencies. A high-yield savings account or a money market account can be a good choice.

3. Automate Savings: One of the most effective ways to build your emergency fund is by automating your savings. Set up automatic transfers from your checking account to your emergency savings account each month. Start with a manageable amount, such as $100

or $200 per month, and gradually increase it as you get used to saving.

4. Cut Back on Expenses: In order to accelerate the growth of your emergency savings fund, consider cutting back on non-essential expenses. This could mean eating out less, canceling subscriptions, or finding more affordable alternatives for your current lifestyle. Redirect the money you save into your emergency fund.

5. Use Windfalls and Bonuses: Whenever you receive unexpected income, such as a tax refund, work bonus, or a gift, consider using a portion of it to add to your emergency fund. This will help you reach your goal faster.

6. Track Your Progress: Keeping track of your progress can be motivating. Set milestones to celebrate along the way, such as hitting the first $1,000 or saving enough for one month's worth of expenses. This will give you a sense of accomplishment and encourage you to keep going.

7. Avoid Using Your Emergency Fund for Non-Emergencies: One of the biggest temptations when building an emergency fund is to dip into it for non-urgent expenses. Resist the urge to use it for vacations, shopping sprees, or home improvements. Your emergency fund should be reserved only for true emergencies, such as job loss, medical bills, or essential home repairs.

Where to Keep Your Emergency Savings Fund

Choosing where to keep your emergency savings fund is just as important as saving it in the first place. You want your funds to be easily accessible, but not so accessible that you spend them on non-emergencies.

1. High-Yield Savings Accounts: A high-yield savings account offers a better interest rate than a traditional savings account, allowing your emergency fund to grow over time. These accounts are often offered by online banks and may require a minimum balance to open.

2. Money Market Accounts: Money market accounts often offer higher interest rates than savings accounts, though the rates may be slightly lower than those of high-yield savings accounts. They also provide easy access to your funds, though there may be withdrawal limits.

3. Certificates of Deposit (CDs): If you don't need immediate access to your emergency fund, you might consider putting a portion of it in a certificate of deposit (CD). This type of account typically offers higher interest rates but requires you to lock in your money for a set period. However, this option is better suited for individuals with a longer-term savings goal or who can afford to keep their money locked away.

4. Cash in a Safe Place: While it's important to avoid using your emergency savings for non-emergencies, it's also important to ensure it's not so difficult to access that it defeats the purpose. Cash should be stored in a safe, secure place where you can quickly access it when necessary.

Building an emergency savings fund is one of the most important financial steps you can take to ensure long-term financial stability and peace of mind. By setting a realistic savings goal, automating your savings, and resisting the temptation to dip into your fund for non-emergencies, you can create a cushion that helps protect you from life's unexpected financial hurdles.

The journey to building your emergency savings may take time, but the benefits are undeniable. A solid emergency fund provides security and freedom, allowing you to navigate life's challenges without the stress and burden of financial uncertainty. Start today, and take the first step towards building a more secure and financially sound future.

How Much to Save and Where to Keep It

Saving money is an essential step toward achieving financial stability and independence. However, many people struggle with understanding how much to save and where to keep it. These questions are not only about the amount but also about creating the right strategy for managing savings. In this article, we will break down how much you should save, how to calculate your savings goals, and where to store it for optimal growth and security.

How Much Should You Save?

The amount you should save depends on various factors such as your income, lifestyle, financial goals, and long-term aspirations. While there is no one-size-fits-all rule, there are general guidelines that can help you determine a savings target that works for you.

1. The 50/30/20 Rule

A widely recommended approach to saving is the 50/30/20 rule. This rule suggests that:

- 50% of your income should go toward essential living expenses like housing, utilities, groceries, and transportation.
- 30% of your income should be allocated to discretionary expenses

like entertainment, dining out, and hobbies.

- 20% of your income should be dedicated to savings and debt repayment.

This is a general guideline that allows you to live comfortably while also planning for your future. If you have high living expenses or debt, you may need to adjust these percentages to prioritize savings more.

2. Emergency Fund

The first priority for most people when saving is to build an emergency fund. Financial experts recommend saving three to six months' worth of living expenses. An emergency fund acts as a financial cushion during unexpected events such as job loss, medical emergencies, or urgent home repairs.

For example, if your monthly expenses total $3,000, you should aim to save between $9,000 and $18,000 for emergencies. This amount can offer you peace of mind and protect you from falling into debt when facing a financial crisis.

3. Retirement Savings

Another important savings goal is retirement. The earlier you start saving for retirement, the more time your money will have to grow.

For instance, if you earn $50,000 a year, this means setting aside at least $5,000 to $7,500 annually for retirement. If your employer offers a 401(k) with a match, take full advantage of this benefit.

4. Specific Financial Goals

Apart from emergency savings and retirement, you may have other specific financial goals such as purchasing a home, starting a business, or funding your child's education. Each of these goals will require careful planning and saving.

The amount you should save will depend on the goal and the time frame in which you want to achieve it. For example, if you plan to buy a house in five years and need $50,000 for a down payment, you should aim to save $10,000 per year.

5. Debt Repayment

While saving is important, it's also crucial to pay off high-interest debt. If you have credit card debt or payday loans, it's advisable to pay these off first before aggressively saving, especially because interest on these types of debt can quickly outweigh savings growth.

Once you've paid off high-interest debt, you can then focus more on building up your savings. If you have student loans or mortgages, these payments can be managed alongside your savings without too much difficulty.

Where to Keep Your Savings?

Now that we know how much to save, it's equally important to understand where to keep those savings. The right savings vehicle will depend on your goals, your timeline, and your tolerance for risk.

1. Checking and Savings Accounts

For immediate or short-term savings, keeping money in a checking or savings account is a good option. These accounts are accessible, and savings accounts typically offer a small amount of interest, allowing your funds to grow slowly.

- Checking accounts are best for money you need access to regularly.
- Savings accounts are better for storing money that you don't need immediate access to but may want to access quickly in an emergency.

Some savings accounts offer a slightly higher interest rate than others, so it's worth shopping around or using online banks, which tend to offer better interest rates than traditional brick-and-mortar banks.

2. Retirement Accounts

If your primary savings goal is retirement, you should consider using retirement accounts like IRAs or 401(k)s. These accounts offer tax benefits, which can help your savings grow faster. However, the drawback is that you typically cannot access the funds until you reach retirement age without incurring penalties.

- 401(k)s are employer-sponsored plans that may also offer matching contributions, which can significantly boost your savings.
- IRAs (Individual Retirement Accounts) offer individuals a way to save for retirement independently of an employer. IRAs come in two types: Traditional and Roth, each with different tax advantages.

3. Investing for Growth

For long-term savings goals like retirement or buying a home, investing in the stock market can offer a higher return than keeping money in a savings account. However, investing carries risk, and there is no guarantee that your investments will grow.

Common options for long-term investment include mutual funds, index funds, individual stocks, and exchange-traded funds (ETFs). If you are new to investing, consider speaking with a financial advisor to help you make informed decisions based on your goals and risk tolerance.

4. Real Estate

If you are saving for a major purchase like a home or property, real estate can be a smart choice. Real estate is often a long-term investment that can provide both appreciation in value and passive income in the form of rent. However, real estate typically requires a large upfront investment and ongoing maintenance costs.

Saving is a crucial component of financial planning, and knowing how much to save and where to store your funds can make a significant difference in achieving your financial goals. Whether you are building an emergency fund, saving for retirement, or planning for a large purchase, it's important to consider your savings goals and timelines before deciding where to store your money.

Automating Savings to Make It Easier: A Comprehensive Guide

Saving money is a crucial aspect of financial well-being, yet many people struggle to set aside money regularly. One effective strategy to overcome this obstacle is automating savings. By automating the process, you can ensure that money is consistently saved without having to think about it actively. In this article, we'll explore the benefits of automating savings, how to set up automated systems, and tips for making the process work for you.

Why Automating Savings is Essential

Before diving into how to automate savings, let's first understand why it is so beneficial. The concept of automating savings means setting up systems where money is transferred to your savings account or investment vehicles without you manually intervening. It is a smart and efficient way to achieve your financial goals without being distracted by daily spending temptations.

1. Consistency and Discipline: One of the biggest challenges of saving is the lack of consistency. People often save money only when there's extra income or when they remember to do so. Automating your savings eliminates this issue by ensuring that a fixed amount is saved on a regular schedule. This consistency helps build healthy financial habits that lead to long-term wealth accumulation.

2. Less Stress and More Convenience: Life gets busy, and the more you can automate, the less mental energy you'll expend on it. By automating your savings, you don't have to worry about transferring money from your checking account to your savings account every month. This eliminates the risk of missing payments or forgetting to save entirely.

3. Prevents Impulse Spending: When money is sitting in your checking account, it's tempting to spend it on non-essential items. Automating your savings ensures that money is transferred before you even have the chance to spend it. This "paying yourself first" mentality allows you to set aside funds before daily expenses eat away at your resources.

4. Reaches Financial Goals Faster: Automating savings encourages you to save consistently toward your goals. Whether you're building an emergency fund, saving for a down payment on a house, or investing for retirement, automatic savings can help you reach those objectives much faster than sporadic saving. Over time, compounded savings can significantly impact your financial growth.

How to Set Up Automated Savings

Now that you know why automating savings is essential, it's time to look at how to implement this strategy in your life. Here's a step-by-step guide to setting up automated savings:

1. Determine Your Savings Goals

Before you can set up an automated savings plan, you must identify your savings goals. Are you saving for an emergency fund, a vacation, a new car, or retirement? Different goals may require different approaches in terms of how much to save and how quickly you want to reach them. By defining your goals clearly, you'll have a better idea of how much money you need to save and can determine a realistic amount to automate.

2. Set a Fixed Amount to Save

Once your goals are defined, determine how much money you can realistically set aside for savings each month. You can either use a fixed dollar amount, or set a percentage of your income. Some financial experts recommend saving at least 20% of your monthly income, but if that's not feasible for you, start with a smaller amount and gradually increase it.

3. Choose Your Savings Account

Choose a savings account that suits your goals. If you are building an emergency fund, you may want to opt for a high-yield savings account that offers a higher interest rate. If you're saving for retirement, you might consider using an Individual Retirement Account (IRA) or employer-sponsored 401(k) plan. For short-term goals, a regular savings or money market account may be ideal. You'll need to select the account that aligns with your objectives and growth expectations.

4. Set Up Automatic Transfers

Next, set up automatic transfers to your savings account. Most banks and financial institutions allow you to schedule transfers between accounts. You can specify the amount to transfer and the frequency (weekly, bi-weekly, or monthly). The transfer will occur automatically, ensuring that you never miss a deposit. You can also set up recurring transfers through third-party apps or tools, such as PayPal or apps designed for automated savings like Digit or Qapital.

5. Make Use of Employer Direct Deposit

Many employers offer the option to split direct deposit between multiple accounts. If your employer offers this service, you can have a portion of your paycheck directly deposited into your savings account. This is a seamless way to ensure that a portion of your income is saved before you even see it, further reducing the temptation to spend.

6. Take Advantage of Apps and Tools

Today, there are various apps that make automating savings easier. Some apps round up your purchases to the nearest dollar and transfer the change to your savings account. For example, apps like Acorns and Chime automatically round up the cost of your purchases and save the difference. These small increments can add up over time, helping you save effortlessly.

7. Monitor and Adjust Over Time

While automation is an excellent tool for savings, it's essential to monitor your progress and make adjustments if necessary. Over time, your financial situation and goals may change, so it's a good idea to periodically review your savings strategy. If you receive a raise or have extra income, consider increasing your savings amount. Similarly, if your financial situation changes, you may need to adjust the amount you're saving to stay on track.

Tips for Maximizing Your Automated Savings

Now that you know how to set up automated savings, here are a few tips to ensure you get the most out of the process:

1. Automate Your Expenses First

Before automating savings, ensure that you've already set up systems for paying bills and covering essential expenses. The key to success with automated savings is making it a top priority, so automate your bills and expenses first, then allocate a portion of your income for savings.

2. Build Up an Emergency Fund

An emergency fund should be your first priority when automating savings. Having an emergency fund (typically three to six months of living expenses) can protect you against unforeseen circumstances like job loss, medical emergencies, or car repairs. This fund gives you the peace of mind to continue saving for other goals without fear of dipping into your savings.

3. Track Your Progress

Use tools such as budgeting apps or spreadsheets to track how much you've saved. Keeping an eye on your progress will help you stay motivated and allow you to see how consistent saving impacts your financial situation. Apps like Mint or YNAB (You Need a Budget) can be used to track your savings alongside your spending.

4. Avoid the Urge to Withdraw

When saving automatically, you may be tempted to withdraw the money for non-emergencies. To avoid this, keep your savings account separate from your checking account. The further away your savings are from your day-to-day spending habits, the less likely you are to dip into them.

5. Set Milestones

Celebrate when you reach certain milestones, such as saving your first $1,000 or hitting 50% of your savings goal. This helps maintain motivation and reminds you of the progress you've made. Positive reinforcement encourages continued savings.

Automating savings is one of the simplest yet most effective ways to achieve financial stability and reach your financial goals. By setting up automated transfers, choosing the right savings tools, and staying committed to the process, you can save consistently and reach your financial goals more efficiently. It may take time to see significant results, but the beauty of automated savings is that it allows you to make progress toward your financial goals without constant effort or thought. Embrace automation, and you'll be on your way to building a secure financial future.

Cutting Debt and Saving

In today's fast-paced world, managing finances can feel overwhelming. With growing expenses and an ever-increasing debt load, many individuals find themselves struggling to stay afloat financially. However, there is hope. By implementing strategic steps to cut debt and save effectively, you can take control of your financial future and work towards achieving long-term financial security.

Understanding Debt

Before diving into debt reduction strategies, it's important to understand the different types of debt:

1. Secured Debt – This includes loans where assets (such as homes or cars) are used as collateral. Mortgages and auto loans are examples of secured debt.

2. Unsecured Debt – This includes loans or credit that are not tied to any asset. Credit card debt, student loans, and medical bills fall under this category.

3. Revolving Debt – Credit cards and lines of credit are examples of revolving debt. You are allowed to borrow and repay repeatedly, up to a specified limit.

4. Installment Debt – This includes loans with fixed payments over a set period, such as personal loans and car loans.

Steps to Cutting Debt

1. Create a Budget

A budget is your financial roadmap. It will help you understand how much money you're bringing in, how much you're spending, and where you can make adjustments. Create a list of your income sources and monthly expenses, and allocate funds toward debt repayment. Track your spending to ensure you're sticking to your budget.

2. Prioritize High-Interest Debt

When it comes to paying down debt, prioritize high-interest debt first. Credit cards, for example, often have high-interest rates that can quickly accumulate. Focus on paying off these debts faster to save on interest payments. Once a high-interest debt is paid off, move on to the next one.

3. Consolidate or Refinance Debt

If you have multiple high-interest debts, consider consolidating them into one loan or refinancing to get a lower interest rate. This can simplify your payments and reduce the overall amount of interest you'll pay.

4. Cut Unnecessary Expenses

Examine your monthly spending and identify areas where you can cut back. Whether it's dining out less often, reducing subscriptions, or finding cheaper alternatives for everyday items, trimming these expenses can free up extra funds to put towards debt repayment.

5. Increase Your Income

Look for opportunities to increase your income, whether through a side job, freelance work, or selling items you no longer need. Any extra income can help accelerate your debt repayment process.

Steps to Saving Effectively

1. Set Clear Financial Goals

Start by determining your financial objectives. Do you want to build an emergency fund, save for a vacation, or invest for retirement? Setting specific goals will help guide your savings plan.

2. Pay Yourself First

Before paying bills or making discretionary purchases, prioritize saving. Set up automatic transfers to a savings account, even if it's a small amount. This ensures that saving becomes a habit, rather than an afterthought.

3. Build an Emergency Fund

Aim to save at least three to six months' worth of living expenses in an emergency fund. This provides a safety net in case of unexpected events like job loss or medical emergencies, reducing the need to rely on credit cards or loans in difficult times.

4. Live Below Your Means

One of the most effective ways to save money is to spend less than you earn. By making mindful choices and living below your means, you'll free up more funds to put toward savings and investments. It's not about depriving yourself, but about finding balance and making thoughtful decisions with your money.

5. Automate Your Savings

Set up automatic contributions to your savings or retirement accounts. This makes it easier to save consistently without the temptation to spend that money elsewhere.

6. Take Advantage of Employer Benefits

Many employers offer matching contributions for retirement plans like 401(k)s. If your employer offers this benefit, make sure you're contributing enough to take full advantage of the match. It's essentially free money that can help grow your retirement savings.

7. Invest for the Future

Once you've built your emergency fund and are saving consistently, consider investing for long-term goals, like retirement. Diversify your investment portfolio by investing in stocks, bonds, mutual funds, or real estate to help grow your wealth over time.

Creating a Financial Plan

The key to financial success lies in a clear, well-structured financial plan. This includes:

- Assessing your current financial situation by evaluating your assets, debts, and income.
- Setting short-term and long-term goals for savings, debt reduction, and investment.
- Implementing the strategies outlined in this guide for cutting debt

and saving effectively.

- Reviewing and adjusting your plan regularly to ensure you're on track.

Cutting debt and saving money takes discipline, patience, and consistency, but with the right approach, you can achieve financial freedom. By prioritizing your debt repayment, living below your means, and automating your savings, you'll build a strong financial foundation that will support you for years to come. Remember, financial freedom isn't just about eliminating debt—it's about creating a life where you can enjoy peace of mind and financial security.

Stay committed to your goals, and you'll find yourself on the path to long-term financial success.

The Impact of Debt on Savings and How to Reduce It

Debt is an inevitable part of modern life. Whether it's student loans, mortgages, car payments, or credit card balances, most people at some point take on some form of debt. While debt can help finance important purchases or investments, it can have a significant negative impact on savings. The relationship between debt and savings is complex and understanding how debt affects savings is crucial for financial well-being.

Let's explores the impact of debt on savings and offers actionable strategies to reduce debt and improve savings.

The Impact of Debt on Savings

1. Interest Payments Draining Resources

One of the most direct ways debt affects savings is through interest payments. When you borrow money, you are not just paying back the principal amount but also paying interest on the borrowed sum. Interest payments often increase the total amount owed, leaving borrowers with less money to put towards savings. For example, credit card debt typically carries high-interest rates, meaning borrowers could pay off only a fraction of the principal each month, while the rest is eaten up by interest payments. This leaves less room for individuals to contribute to savings accounts or retirement funds, hindering long-term financial stability.

2. Opportunity Cost of Paying Off Debt

Debt can also lead to opportunity costs. When you allocate a significant portion of your monthly income to paying off debt, you may miss out on opportunities to invest or save for future goals, such as retirement, a child's education, or a down payment on a home. For instance, contributing to a retirement fund like a 401(k) or an IRA often results in immediate tax advantages and long-term wealth building. However, if a substantial portion of your income is going towards paying off high-interest debts, you might forgo these opportunities, potentially missing out on the long-term growth that compound interest offers.

3. Debt Compounds Financial Stress

Another critical impact of debt on savings is the psychological and emotional toll it can take. Constantly worrying about debt can create stress and anxiety, which may negatively affect financial decision-making. People under financial stress might be less likely to stick to a budget or may make impulsive decisions that lead to even greater debt. Furthermore, individuals who are stressed about their financial situation may have difficulty focusing on long-term goals like saving and investing. In such cases, debt does not only affect savings directly but can also impair one's ability to plan for a secure financial future.

4. Credit Score and Future Borrowing

Carrying high levels of debt can also negatively impact your credit score, which is a crucial factor when applying for loans or credit cards. If your credit score drops because of accumulated debt, you may not be eligible for favorable interest rates on loans. This means that if you need to borrow money for a home, car, or education in the future, you may end up paying significantly higher interest rates, which in turn increases your financial burden and reduces the amount you can save or invest. Low credit scores often lead to higher borrowing costs, further delaying your ability to build savings.

5. Limited Financial Flexibility

Debt can limit your financial flexibility. If a large portion of your income is committed to paying down debt, it becomes more difficult to handle unexpected expenses, like medical bills, car repairs, or job loss. This could lead to additional borrowing or reliance on high-interest loans, creating a vicious cycle of debt. Moreover, individuals who are heavily in debt often find themselves unable to take advantage of opportunities, such as moving to a higher-paying job or purchasing property, because they don't have the financial freedom to make such choices. This restricts their ability to build wealth and savings.

How to Reduce Debt and Improve Savings

1. Create a Budget and Stick to It

The first step to managing and reducing debt is creating a comprehensive budget. This budget should detail all income sources, expenses, and debt obligations. By tracking income and expenditures, you can identify areas where you can cut back and allocate more money toward debt repayment. The more you can reduce discretionary spending, the more you can direct toward paying off high-interest debts. This process not only helps you reduce debt but also ensures that your savings rate increases over time.

2. Pay Off High-Interest Debt First

One of the most effective ways to reduce debt is by paying off high-interest debts first. These debts, such as credit cards, often carry much higher rates than other types of loans, such as mortgages or student loans. Paying off high-interest debt can free up more of your income, allowing you to save and invest more in the future. The "debt avalanche" method involves paying off the highest-interest debt first while making minimum payments on other debts. Once the high-interest debt is paid off, you can shift the funds to the next highest-interest debt, and so on.

3. Consolidate or Refinance Debt

If you have multiple debts with high interest rates, consolidating them into one loan with a lower interest rate could help you pay off your debt faster and save on interest payments. Similarly, refinancing options for student loans or mortgages can lower monthly payments and free up funds for saving. If you're considering refinancing or consolidation, it's essential to shop around for the best rates and understand the terms involved to ensure that the move will save you money in the long run.

4. Build an Emergency Fund

One of the most important steps to breaking the cycle of debt is establishing an emergency fund. This fund acts as a buffer against unexpected expenses, so you don't have to rely on credit cards or loans when an emergency arises. Ideally, an emergency fund should cover three to six months' worth of living expenses. With an emergency fund in place, you'll be less likely to fall deeper into debt during financial setbacks, and you'll be able to maintain a steady savings routine without interruption.

5. Set Clear Financial Goals

Setting clear, achievable financial goals is key to staying motivated in your journey toward debt reduction and saving. Whether your goal is to pay off a certain amount of debt in six months or save a specific amount for retirement, defining your financial objectives helps create a roadmap. Break down large goals into smaller, manageable steps, and celebrate milestones along the way. Clear goals also help you stay focused and make better financial decisions that align with your long-term financial vision.

6. Consider Financial Counseling

If you find yourself overwhelmed by debt and unable to develop a strategy for repayment and saving, seeking professional financial counseling may be beneficial. Financial counselors can help you create a plan that fits your unique financial situation and provide strategies for reducing debt, improving credit, and saving money. A counselor may also suggest resources or programs that can help consolidate your debt or negotiate better terms with creditors.

7. Adopt a Mindful Approach to Spending

Finally, adopting a more mindful approach to spending can make a big difference in reducing debt and increasing savings. Evaluate your spending habits and ask yourself if each purchase aligns with your values and goals. Mindful spending doesn't mean depriving yourself, but it encourages you to prioritize your needs over wants and make thoughtful, intentional financial decisions. Cutting out unnecessary expenses can create more room in your budget for debt repayment and saving.

Debt, when left unmanaged, can have a significant impact on savings and overall financial health. The interest payments, the opportunity costs, and the stress that debt brings can hinder your ability to save and invest in the future. However, by developing a clear plan to reduce debt, being mindful of your financial habits, and prioritizing saving, it's possible to break free from the cycle of debt and start building a solid financial foundation. It takes time and discipline, but with commitment and the right strategies, financial freedom and the ability to build wealth are achievable.

The Snowball vs. Avalanche Method for Paying Off Debt

When it comes to paying off debt, two popular strategies often arise: the Snowball Method and the Avalanche Method. Both approaches offer their own advantages, and understanding the nuances of each can help you decide which one best suits your financial situation and goals. While the ultimate goal is the same—freedom from debt—the way to achieve it can vary depending on your priorities.

The Snowball Method: Building Momentum

The Snowball Method is a debt repayment strategy where you focus on paying off your smallest debt first, regardless of interest rates. Once the smallest debt is paid off, you move on to the next smallest, and so on, until all debts are cleared.

How It Works

1. List Your Debts: Begin by listing all of your debts, excluding the interest rate. Instead, focus solely on the amount owed. You can include credit cards, student loans, personal loans, or any other forms of debt.

2. Minimum Payments: Make the minimum payments on all debts, except for the smallest one. For the smallest debt, put as much extra money toward it as possible.

3. Pay Off the Smallest Debt: Once the smallest debt is paid off, take the money you were putting toward that debt and apply it to the next smallest debt.

4. Repeat the Process: Continue this process until all debts are paid off.

Advantages of the Snowball Method

1. Psychological Wins: One of the most significant benefits of the Snowball Method is the psychological boost it provides. By paying off smaller debts quickly, you get to experience the sense of accomplishment and relief that can come with eliminating a debt. This positive reinforcement can help keep you motivated throughout the process.

2. Easier to Stay Committed: Paying off a smaller debt may feel more manageable and attainable, reducing feelings of overwhelm. The quicker wins may inspire a sense of momentum that helps you stick with the plan.

3. Increased Confidence: Each time a debt is paid off, you'll feel more empowered to take on the next one. Over time, this confidence can

propel you to tackle larger debts, even when the road gets tough.

Disadvantages of the Snowball Method

1. Not the Most Cost-Effective: The Snowball Method doesn't always save the most money in the long run. By focusing on the smallest debt, you could end up paying more in interest on larger debts with higher interest rates, which means you might take longer to pay off everything and pay more overall.

2. Slow Progress on High-Interest Debt: If your largest debts carry high interest, such as credit cards, the Snowball Method can slow down your progress in paying them off. The interest on these debts may keep accruing while you're focused on your smaller debts, increasing the amount of debt you ultimately owe.

The Avalanche Method: Paying Off Debt Efficiently

The Avalanche Method takes a more mathematical approach to paying off debt. Instead of focusing on the size of the debt, you prioritize paying off the debts with the highest interest rates first, regardless of the balance. This approach reduces the overall interest paid and allows you to become debt-free in less time.

How It Works

1. List Your Debts by Interest Rate: Write down all of your debts and list them from highest to lowest interest rate, rather than from smallest to largest balance.

2. Minimum Payments: Continue making the minimum payments on all of your debts, except for the one with the highest interest rate. Put as much extra money as possible toward this high-interest debt.

3. Pay Off the Debt with the Highest Interest Rate: Once the highest-interest debt is paid off, apply the funds you were using to it to the next debt with the highest interest rate, and continue the process.

4. Repeat the Process: Continue this process until all debts are paid off.

Advantages of the Avalanche Method

1. Saves Money in Interest: The most significant benefit of the Avalanche Method is that it minimizes the amount of interest you pay over time. By focusing on the high-interest debts first, you reduce the total amount paid, allowing more of your payment to go toward the principal balance rather than the interest.

2. Quicker Debt Repayment: Because the Avalanche Method reduces the total interest paid, you may be able to pay off your debts faster. Without high-interest charges accruing, you can focus on reducing the principal of your debts more efficiently.

3. Financially Optimal: In the long term, the Avalanche Method will save you the most money and help you pay off your debts quicker. This is the mathematically sound choice, especially if you're focused on financial efficiency.

Disadvantages of the Avalanche Method

1. Slower Psychological Progress: One of the downsides of the Avalanche Method is that it doesn't offer the immediate gratification that the Snowball Method provides. Paying off large debts with high interest may take longer, which could feel discouraging at first.

2. Potential for Reduced Motivation: The Avalanche Method requires

you to stay focused for longer periods, especially when tackling larger debts. Without the psychological victories of eliminating smaller debts, you might feel less motivated to continue.

3. Difficult to Stay on Track: Because of the slow progress on high-interest debts, some people may become frustrated and quit before completing the process, particularly if they don't see quick results.

Which Method is Best for You?

The Snowball Method and the Avalanche Method are both valid strategies for paying off debt, and choosing between them depends on your personal preferences, goals, and circumstances. If you need quick wins to stay motivated and build momentum, the Snowball Method might be the right choice for you. It's especially useful for individuals who struggle with staying motivated or feel overwhelmed by large amounts of debt.

However, if your goal is to minimize the amount of interest you pay over time and pay off your debts as quickly as possible, the Avalanche Method is likely the better option. This approach is especially beneficial for people who are financially driven and can handle the longer-term commitment of tackling large debts first.

Some people even combine both strategies by using the Snowball Method for smaller debts, while simultaneously focusing on high-interest debts to minimize interest charges. This hybrid method can offer both the psychological benefits of the Snowball Method and the financial efficiency of the Avalanche Method.

Both the Snowball and Avalanche methods offer a systematic way to get out of debt, and the best method for you ultimately depends on what motivates you most. If you prefer emotional wins and rapid progress, the Snowball Method may be the right fit. On the other hand, if your priority is to save money on interest and pay off your debts as efficiently as possible, the Avalanche Method is likely a better strategy. No matter which approach you choose, the important thing is to stay committed, make steady progress, and take control of your financial future.

How Clearing Debt Improves Your Ability to Save

Debt is a financial burden that can weigh heavily on your ability to achieve financial goals, including saving. Whether it's credit card debt, student loans, personal loans, or other types of liabilities, the burden of debt can create a sense of financial instability. Clearing debt, however, can significantly improve your ability to save and build wealth over time. In this article, we'll explore how clearing debt can help you save more, reduce financial stress, and set you on the path to long-term financial success.

The Financial Strain of Debt

Before we explore the positive impact of clearing debt, it's important to understand the challenges debt presents. Debt comes with interest payments, monthly dues, and an overall reduction in disposable income. The interest on credit cards, for example, can be particularly debilitating, often exceeding 20% or more annually. When your monthly income is spent servicing these debts, the amount of money you can allocate to savings becomes minimal.

Debt can also restrict your financial flexibility. For instance, if a large portion of your paycheck is directed toward servicing loans or credit card balances, you may be left with very little for unexpected expenses or savings contributions. Debt can keep you living paycheck to paycheck, preventing you from setting aside money for emergencies, investments, or retirement.

The Role of Debt in Reducing Your Savings Potential

One of the primary ways debt hinders your ability to save is by occupying a large portion of your income. For instance, if you have monthly payments on several credit cards, personal loans, or mortgages, a significant portion of your earnings goes toward paying interest and reducing the principal balances. As a result, this limits the amount of money you have left to allocate to a savings account or other investment vehicles.

The more debt you have, the more your money is tied up in paying off liabilities, leaving less room to prioritize savings. This is especially true when the interest rates on your debts are high, as you may be paying more in interest than you are able to put away in savings each month. In fact, many people with significant debt find it challenging to even begin saving for an emergency fund, retirement, or other long-term financial goals.

Benefits of Clearing Debt

Clearing debt can have a profound effect on your financial well-being and your ability to save. Let's explore the benefits in more detail.

1. Increased Disposable Income
   One of the most immediate benefits of paying off debt is an increase

in your disposable income. Once you've cleared high-interest credit card debt or loans, the money that was previously allocated toward monthly payments becomes available for savings. For example, if you were paying $400 each month toward credit card bills, that same amount could now be redirected to an emergency fund or retirement account.

The more debt you pay off, the more money you free up for savings. As you reduce or eliminate debt, the percentage of your income available to fund savings and investments grows, making it easier to prioritize your financial future.

2. Reduced Financial Stress

Debt can cause significant stress and anxiety. When you're constantly worried about making payments, facing high interest rates, or dealing with late fees, it can be difficult to think about long-term financial goals, such as saving for a home or retirement. Once you clear your debt, you free yourself from the mental burden of financial stress.

When you're no longer bogged down by debt, you can focus your energy on planning for your future and growing your savings. The peace of mind that comes with financial freedom allows you to approach saving with a clear and calm mindset, which can ultimately lead to better financial decisions.

3. Improved Credit Score

Clearing debt also improves your credit score. Your credit score is an important factor when applying for loans, credit cards, or even renting an apartment. Having a high credit score can also result in lower interest rates when you do borrow money in the future. By eliminating debt, you reduce your credit utilization ratio and demonstrate your ability to manage finances responsibly, which can boost your credit score over time.

A higher credit score can lower the cost of borrowing in the future, freeing up more of your income to save. It can also improve your chances of qualifying for favorable loans or credit terms, which may be beneficial when making large purchases or investing.

4. Increased Financial Flexibility

As you clear debt, you gain greater financial flexibility. With fewer liabilities weighing you down, you have more room to make choices that align with your financial goals. Whether you want to invest in the stock market, save for a major life event, or contribute more to your retirement account, clearing debt creates space in your budget for those goals.

Furthermore, as you eliminate debt, you may be able to put more money toward savings without sacrificing your lifestyle. Having more flexibility in your finances gives you the freedom to choose how to allocate your money to achieve your goals.

5. Long-Term Financial Security

The ultimate goal of clearing debt is to achieve long-term financial security. When you eliminate liabilities and start building savings, you create a solid foundation for your financial future. Saving consistently over time allows you to build an emergency fund, invest for retirement, and reach other important financial goals.

Having savings in place provides a financial cushion that can protect you during challenging times, such as job loss or medical emergencies. Instead of relying on credit cards or loans to cover unexpected expenses, you can tap into your savings and avoid accumulating more debt.

How to Start Clearing Debt and Building Savings

Now that we understand how clearing debt can improve your ability to save, it's important to know how to take the first step. Here are some practical strategies to help you get started:

1. Create a Budget: The first step in eliminating debt and building savings is understanding your income and expenses. Create a budget that tracks your spending, identifies areas for cutbacks, and allows you to allocate more money toward paying off debt.

2. Pay Off High-Interest Debt First: Focus on paying off high-interest debt, such as credit cards, before tackling lower-interest loans. The interest on credit cards can quickly accumulate, making it more difficult to pay down the balance.

3. Build an Emergency Fund: Even while paying off debt, try to set aside some money for emergencies. Having a small emergency fund can prevent you from relying on credit cards or loans when unexpected expenses arise.

4. Automate Savings: Once your debt is under control, automate your savings. Set up automatic transfers to a savings account or retirement fund so you're consistently building wealth without thinking about it.

5. Avoid Accumulating More Debt: As you work to clear your current debt, be mindful not to accumulate more. Avoid impulsive purchases, limit credit card use, and focus on living within your means.

Clearing debt is an essential step in improving your financial health and increasing your ability to save. By eliminating the financial burden of monthly payments and high interest rates, you can free up more of your income for savings, reduce financial stress, and set yourself up for long-term financial success. The process may take time, but the benefits of being debt-free are well worth the effort. Once your debts are cleared, you'll have the financial flexibility and peace of mind to build wealth, invest in your future, and live a life of financial security.

Saving For Big Goals

Saving for big goals is an essential step in achieving your dreams, whether it's buying a home, starting a business, going on a dream vacation, or retiring comfortably. However, reaching these big goals requires careful planning, discipline, and a structured approach to saving.

Here's a breakdown of how to save for your significant goals:

1. Define Your Goal

Before you start saving, it's important to clearly define your goal. The more specific you can be, the better. For example, instead of saying, "I want to save for a house," you could say, "I want to save $50,000 for a down payment on a house in 5 years." This gives you a target to work toward and helps make the savings process more tangible.

2. Set a Timeline

Determine a realistic timeline for achieving your goal. For example, if you're saving for a $10,000 vacation, you can set a goal to have that money saved within the next two years. Setting a clear timeline helps you determine how much you need to save each month to stay on track.

3. Create a Budget

A budget is your financial blueprint. By tracking your income and expenses, you can identify areas where you can cut back and allocate that money toward your goal. Creating and sticking to a budget allows you to prioritize your big goal while managing everyday expenses.

4. Open a Dedicated Savings Account

It's easier to save if you keep your savings separate from your spending money. Consider opening a dedicated savings account specifically for your big goal. This helps you resist the temptation to dip into the savings for everyday purchases. Look into high-interest savings accounts or CDs for your big goal to earn a little extra as you save.

5. Automate Your Savings

To make saving effortless, consider automating your savings. You can set up a direct deposit to transfer a fixed amount into your dedicated savings account each month. This "pay yourself first" mentality ensures that you are consistently contributing to your goal without having to think about it.

6. Track Your Progress

Regularly monitor your savings progress. By checking in with your goal periodically, you can assess whether you're on track or if adjustments need to be made. Tracking progress can be motivating as you see your savings grow.

7. Cut Back on Non-Essentials

If you find that you're not saving as quickly as you'd like, look at ways to reduce discretionary spending. Consider cutting back on dining out, entertainment, or shopping. The more you can trim from your expenses, the faster you'll be able to reach your goal.

8. Increase Your Income

Sometimes, the best way to reach a big financial goal is by increasing your income. Look for opportunities to take on a side job, freelance work, or sell unused items. A temporary boost in income can give your savings a major push toward reaching your goal faster.

9. Stay Motivated

Saving for a big goal can take time, and there may be moments of frustration. Stay motivated by reminding yourself of the purpose behind your goal. Break it into smaller milestones, and celebrate when you reach each one to keep your spirits high.

10. Prepare for Setbacks

Life can be unpredictable, and unexpected expenses may arise. It's important to be flexible with your savings strategy and adjust your plan when necessary. Building an emergency fund to cover unforeseen costs can help you stay on track without derailing your goal.

Saving for big goals takes time, commitment, and discipline. But by being strategic with your savings plan, you can achieve the financial milestones that are most important to you. With careful budgeting, automation, and tracking, the road to your big goal becomes more manageable. Take one step at a time, and soon enough, you'll be celebrating the accomplishment of your dreams.

Setting Realistic Goals: House, Education, and Retirement

Saving money is a critical skill that enables financial independence, security, and the fulfillment of long-term dreams. Whether you're looking to purchase a house, pay for your child's education, or secure your retirement, setting realistic financial goals is key to making these aspirations achievable. In this guide, we'll explore how to set practical goals for saving money in three of the most common areas: home ownership, education, and retirement.

1. Setting a Goal for Purchasing a House

Owning a home is a dream for many, but without proper financial planning, it can feel out of reach. Setting a realistic savings goal for a house requires understanding several factors, including home prices in your area, the amount needed for a down payment, and ongoing homeownership costs.

- Determine the Price Range: Start by researching home prices in your desired location. Keep in mind that home prices fluctuate depending on the economy, the housing market, and the region you're interested in. It's important to establish a target price for the home you want while being mindful of your budget.

- Saving for a Down Payment: Traditionally, a down payment of 20% of the home price is recommended. However, first-time buyers can often purchase with as little as 3% to 5% down, though this may come with additional fees or private mortgage insurance (PMI). Setting a down payment goal involves saving a percentage of the home price.

- Consider Additional Costs: In addition to the down payment, there are closing costs, inspections, insurance, and moving expenses to consider. These can add thousands of dollars to your home buying expenses, so it's crucial to budget for them as well.

- Create a Timeline: Once you've identified your target home price and down payment goal, break it down into monthly savings. For instance, if you want to save $60,000 over the next five years, you'll need to save $1,000 a month. Be realistic about your income and expenses, and set a timeline that feels achievable.

- Track Progress: Regularly review your progress and make adjustments as necessary. Life events can throw off your plans, but flexibility can ensure that you're still on track.

2. Saving for Education

Education, whether it's for your children or yourself, is a significant expense that requires long-term planning and foresight. Higher education costs have been rising steadily, so setting realistic goals for saving for college is essential.

- Determine the Cost of Education: Research the estimated cost of tuition, room and board, textbooks, and other associated costs at the colleges you're considering. Don't forget to factor in potential price increases over the years. According to the College Board, tuition and fees at private colleges for the 2020-2021 school year averaged $41,000, while public in-state colleges averaged around $10,000. Knowing the total cost will help you set a precise savings goal.

- Start Early: The earlier you begin saving, the more time your money will have to grow through compound interest. Consider setting up a 529 College Savings Plan, which offers tax advantages for education savings. Starting early allows you to take advantage of market growth and reduces the amount you need to save monthly as time progresses.

- Estimate the Amount Needed: To estimate how much to save, divide the total amount needed by the number of years until the student starts college. If a child is 5 years old and the estimated cost of education is $150,000 in 13 years, you would need to save around $900 a month, assuming moderate investment returns. Keep in mind that scholarships, grants, and financial aid may reduce the amount you need to save.

- Include Additional Expenses: Besides tuition, education costs include textbooks, travel expenses, and housing. These expenses can vary depending on the type of school and location. It's also important to take into account inflation—education costs have increased by an average of 5% per year over the past several decades.

- Review Your Financial Aid Options: Even if you're saving diligently, it's important to research available financial aid opportunities. Scholarships, grants, and work-study programs can provide significant financial relief. This could mean you won't need to save as much, but still plan for unforeseen gaps in funding.

3. Retirement Savings Goals

Planning for retirement may feel like a far-off concern, but the earlier you begin saving, the easier it will be to meet your retirement goals. Setting realistic retirement goals requires an understanding of your current lifestyle, desired retirement income, and the role of various retirement savings accounts.

- Estimate Your Retirement Needs: Start by estimating how much money you'll need to live comfortably during retirement. Financial advisors typically recommend saving enough to replace 70% to 80% of your pre-retirement income, though this varies based on your desired lifestyle. For example, if you plan to retire at 65 and anticipate needing $50,000 a year in retirement, you would need 1.25 million if you're aiming for 25 years of retirement.

- Start Saving Early: Time is the most powerful tool when it comes to retirement savings. The earlier you begin saving, the more time your investments have to grow. This allows you to take advantage of compound interest, where the interest earned on your savings begins to earn its own interest.

- Contribute to Retirement Accounts: Take advantage of tax-deferred retirement accounts such as a 401(k) or an IRA. Many employers offer 401(k) matching, which is essentially free money. Contribute enough to take full advantage of this match. Consider working with a financial planner to create a retirement portfolio that aligns with your risk tolerance and retirement timeline.

- Adjust Your Savings Based on Lifestyle: You may want to adjust your savings goal based on your future retirement plans. If you plan to travel extensively or live in an area with a high cost of living, your required retirement savings may be higher than the average. Conversely, if you're looking to live modestly in retirement, your needs may be lower.

- Monitor and Adjust Your Plan: Life changes, and so will your financial situation. Regularly review your retirement plan to ensure that your savings are on track. You may need to adjust your contributions as your salary increases or decreases, or if unexpected expenses arise.

Setting realistic financial goals for purchasing a house, funding education, and securing retirement requires careful planning and dedication. It's essential to start by defining your goals clearly and breaking them down into manageable steps. Regularly tracking your progress and adjusting your plans when necessary will ensure that you stay on track. With patience, discipline, and a clear strategy, you can successfully achieve your financial goals and secure a brighter future for yourself and your loved ones.

The Role of Investment Accounts and Other Financial Tools

Saving money is an essential part of building long-term financial security, and there are numerous ways to do so. While traditional savings accounts are commonly used, investment accounts and other financial tools provide more diverse options for saving and growing wealth. These tools offer potential benefits such as higher returns, tax advantages, and portfolio diversification, which are not available with basic savings accounts. Understanding how investment accounts and financial tools work is key to making informed decisions for your personal financial growth.

1. Investment Accounts: A Key Element in Wealth Building

Investment accounts allow individuals to put their money into various assets, such as stocks, bonds, and mutual funds, with the goal of generating a return over time. These accounts serve as a powerful tool for saving, as they often offer much higher interest rates and growth potential compared to traditional savings accounts. The main investment accounts include individual brokerage accounts, retirement accounts (such as 401(k)s and IRAs), and college savings accounts (like 529 plans).

Brokerage Accounts

Brokerage accounts are among the most common types of investment accounts. Through these accounts, investors can buy and sell various securities like stocks, bonds, mutual funds, and exchange-traded funds (ETFs). The primary advantage of a brokerage account is its flexibility. Investors have the ability to control their investment choices and can buy and sell assets at any time.

Unlike savings accounts, which offer a fixed and low interest rate, brokerage accounts offer the potential for substantial returns based on the performance of the assets chosen. However, these accounts come with risks as well, as the value of investments can fluctuate with market conditions. Therefore, while they provide higher earning potential, they also involve the risk of losing money.

Retirement Accounts (401(k), IRA, Roth IRA)

Retirement accounts are specifically designed to help individuals save for their retirement years. Popular examples include 401(k) plans provided by employers and individual retirement accounts (IRAs). Contributions to these accounts are often made before taxes are deducted, which means individuals pay less in taxes upfront, allowing them to save more.

There are also Roth IRAs, which work in reverse; contributions are made with after-tax income, but withdrawals in retirement are tax-free. These accounts are ideal for people looking for long-term growth and are subject to specific contribution limits and rules. The key benefit of retirement accounts is the compounding growth over time, which allows savings to grow faster than in a traditional savings account.

College Savings Accounts (529 Plans)

College savings plans, or 529 plans, are investment accounts specifically designed for saving for a child's education. Contributions to 529 plans grow tax-deferred, and withdrawals are tax-free as long as the funds are used for qualified education expenses. This provides a significant advantage over taxable accounts, as it allows for more growth without being taxed.

529 plans offer a variety of investment options, including age-based portfolios, which automatically adjust the asset allocation based on the child's age. These plans help families save for future educational costs while providing them with the potential to grow their savings in the stock and bond markets.

2. Financial Tools for Building Wealth

In addition to investment accounts, several financial tools can help individuals save and manage their money more effectively. These tools can work in tandem with investment accounts to enhance overall wealth-building strategies.

High-Yield Savings Accounts

While high-yield savings accounts are similar to traditional savings accounts, they typically offer a much higher interest rate, often several times higher than standard bank accounts. These accounts are great for short-term savings, such as emergency funds or saving for a large purchase, and they still provide easy access to the money.

The main advantage of a high-yield savings account is the ability to earn more interest on your money without taking on any significant risk. While these accounts do not provide the same growth potential as investment accounts, they are a safe and secure place to store money while earning interest.

Certificates of Deposit (CDs)

A certificate of deposit (CD) is a type of savings account offered by banks that requires the depositor to leave their money in the account for a set period, ranging from a few months to several years. In exchange for locking in the money for the term, the bank offers a higher interest rate than a standard savings account.

CDs are considered low-risk investments and are insured by the FDIC, meaning that the deposit is protected up to $250,000. However, if the money is withdrawn before the term ends, the account holder may face penalties. For individuals looking for a safe and predictable way to save and grow their money, a CD can be an attractive option.

Bonds

Bonds are debt securities that governments or corporations issue to raise capital. When you buy a bond, you are essentially lending your money to the issuer in exchange for regular interest payments and the return of your principal investment at maturity. Bonds can be a useful tool for conservative investors seeking lower-risk, steady returns.

There are several types of bonds, including government bonds (such as U.S. Treasury bonds) and corporate bonds. The key benefit of bonds is that they are typically less volatile than stocks, making them a good way to balance risk in a diversified portfolio. For individuals who are saving for retirement or other long-term goals, adding bonds to a portfolio can offer stability and income.

Exchange-Traded Funds (ETFs) and Mutual Funds

ETFs and mutual funds are investment vehicles that pool together money from multiple investors to buy a diversified portfolio of stocks, bonds, or other securities. These funds offer a way to achieve diversification, which can help reduce risk while providing the opportunity for growth.

Mutual funds are actively or passively managed and can invest in various asset classes. ETFs, on the other hand, typically track an index and trade on the stock exchange like individual stocks. Both ETFs and mutual funds provide an easy and cost-effective way to invest in a wide range of assets without having to pick individual stocks.

3. Why Investment Accounts and Financial Tools Matter

Investment accounts and financial tools play a crucial role in building wealth, saving for long-term goals, and achieving financial independence. By utilizing a combination of different accounts and tools, individuals can maximize their savings, reduce their tax liability, and take advantage of the power of compounding returns.

Investment accounts such as brokerage accounts and retirement funds allow individuals to invest their money in assets that have the potential for higher returns than traditional savings accounts. Additionally, they offer tax benefits that can further enhance the growth of wealth. On the other hand, financial tools such as high-yield savings accounts, CDs, and bonds provide safer, lower-risk options that are suitable for short-term savings or as a stabilizing element in a diversified portfolio.

The key to successful money management is understanding which tools are right for your unique financial situation. By combining different investment options with strategic planning, individuals can increase their chances of achieving financial independence and security.

Investment accounts and financial tools provide a wide range of opportunities for individuals to save, grow their wealth, and plan for the future. Each tool has its benefits, whether it's the flexibility of a brokerage account, the tax advantages of a 401(k) or Roth IRA, or the stability of a high-yield savings account or bonds. Understanding the strengths and weaknesses of each tool is crucial for making informed decisions that align with your financial goals. With the right strategy and a diversified approach, anyone can take control of their finances and set themselves on the path to long-term financial success.

Creating a Saving Strategy for Big Purchases

When it comes to making big purchases, whether it's a new car, a home, a vacation, or something else entirely, having a clear saving strategy in place is essential. Big purchases often require significant financial preparation, and a well-thought-out plan can help you achieve your goal without compromising your overall financial health. The process of saving for large purchases may seem daunting, but with the right approach, it can be a smooth and achievable task.

Step 1: Set a Clear Goal

The first step in any saving strategy is to clearly define the goal. Without a specific goal in mind, saving for a big purchase can feel aimless and frustrating. Whether you're planning to buy a car, go on an extravagant vacation, or purchase a new home, being clear about your end goal will provide direction and motivation.

To start, calculate the total cost of the item or experience you wish to purchase. Be sure to account for additional costs such as taxes, shipping, or service fees. Having a concrete figure to work toward gives you a target and helps you stay focused.

For example, if you're saving for a car and you've researched prices, you might find that the vehicle you want costs $30,000. In addition to the cost of the car, you'll also need to account for taxes, registration fees, and insurance. Let's say that total comes to $33,000. Your goal is now to save $33,000 within a specific time frame.

Step 2: Establish a Timeline

Setting a timeline is crucial when saving for big purchases. How long do you have to save? Is it six months, a year, or several years? Your timeline will help determine how much you need to save each month to reach your goal.

If you're saving for a big purchase, it's important to consider both your income and your existing financial commitments. For example, if you have credit card debt or student loans, you may want to adjust your timeline or target a smaller purchase. In contrast, if you have a higher income or fewer financial obligations, you may be able to save more quickly.

Let's assume your goal is to purchase a $33,000 car, and you'd like to save for it in one year. Dividing $33,000 by 12 months, you would need to save $2,750 each month to meet your goal.

If that amount seems unmanageable given your current financial situation, don't worry. You can extend the timeline or reevaluate the total cost to make the goal more realistic. For instance, you might extend the saving period to two years, which would require $1,375 per month.

Step 3: Build a Budget

Now that you know how much you need to save and by when, it's time to build a budget that can help you get there. Budgeting is the cornerstone of any successful saving strategy. A budget allows you to allocate funds for specific purposes, track your spending, and identify areas where you can cut back.

Start by listing your sources of income and monthly expenses. Include all necessary living expenses such as rent, utilities, groceries, transportation, insurance, and savings contributions. You can use a budgeting app, spreadsheet, or the envelope system to help you stay organized.

Once you've outlined your expenses, identify areas where you can cut back. For example, maybe you're spending too much on eating out, subscriptions, or impulse shopping. By reducing these non-essential expenses, you can free up more money for your big purchase.

If you can't fully cut back on some expenses, consider finding additional sources of income to speed up your savings process. Side jobs, freelancing, selling unwanted items, or picking up extra shifts at work are all options that can help you save faster.

Step 4: Open a Dedicated Savings Account

When saving for a big purchase, it's essential to keep the money separate from your regular checking account. This will reduce the temptation to spend it and ensure that your savings are protected.

Opening a dedicated savings account for your big purchase allows you to track your progress more easily and keeps the money out of reach for non-essential purchases. Some banks even offer high-yield savings accounts that can help your money grow faster by offering a higher interest rate.

If you're saving for a large purchase that will take several months or years, you may also want to consider a certificate of deposit (CD), which offers a higher interest rate in exchange for locking your money in for a fixed term. CDs can be a great option for long-term savings.

Step 5: Automate Your Savings

One of the easiest ways to stay on track with your savings goal is to automate your contributions. Set up automatic transfers from your checking account to your savings account on a regular basis (weekly, biweekly, or monthly).

By automating your savings, you're essentially "paying yourself first." This ensures that you're consistently saving for your goal, even when life gets busy or you forget to manually transfer the funds.

If possible, try to increase your automated savings as your income grows or as you pay off debt. This will allow you to reach your goal faster and with less effort.

Step 6: Track Your Progress

Tracking your progress is an important part of staying motivated. As you watch your savings grow, you'll feel a sense of accomplishment that will propel you forward.

You can track your savings progress through a spreadsheet, an app, or even a physical chart. Seeing your goal get closer with each deposit is motivating and will keep you focused on reaching your target. If you encounter any setbacks, don't get discouraged—simply adjust your timeline or budget to get back on track.

Step 7: Evaluate Your Options for Financing

While saving for a big purchase, you may decide that you want to explore other options for financing. If you don't want to wait until you've saved the full amount, you may consider financing your purchase through a loan or a credit card.

However, financing comes with its own set of challenges. It's important to understand the interest rates and repayment terms, as well as the impact on your overall financial situation. If you decide to finance, aim to pay off the debt as quickly as possible to avoid high-interest payments.

Alternatively, some retailers and dealerships offer zero-interest financing for a limited time. If you choose to go this route, make sure you can pay off the balance within the promotional period to avoid interest charges.

Step 8: Stay Disciplined and Be Patient

Finally, the key to success when saving for big purchases is discipline. It may take time to reach your goal, but by sticking to your budget, tracking your progress, and making regular contributions, you'll eventually get there.

Remember that big purchases don't have to happen overnight. Being patient and consistent in your saving efforts will allow you to enjoy your purchase without the burden of debt.

Creating a saving strategy for big purchases is a disciplined but achievable goal. By setting a clear goal, establishing a realistic timeline, building a budget, and staying committed to your plan, you can reach your financial targets and make your big purchases without sacrificing financial security. Whether you're saving for a car, home, vacation, or any other major purchase, following these steps will help you plan and execute your savings strategy effectively, allowing you to enjoy your new purchase with peace of mind.

Smart Investing: Growing Your Money

Investing is one of the most powerful ways to build wealth and achieve financial goals. However, many people find it intimidating, not knowing where to start or how to make wise investment decisions. In this guide, we'll explore the basics of smart investing and provide tips to help you grow your money over time.

Understanding the Basics of Investing

At its core, investing involves putting your money into assets with the expectation of generating a return or profit over time. Unlike saving, where your money typically sits in a bank account earning minimal interest, investing allows you to take on more risk for the potential of higher returns.

The first step in smart investing is understanding the various types of investment options available. These include:

1. Stocks – Buying shares of companies allows you to own a piece of the business. Stocks have the potential for high returns but come with

higher risk due to market fluctuations.

2. Bonds – Bonds are essentially loans that you give to companies or governments in exchange for regular interest payments. They are considered lower risk than stocks but offer more modest returns.

3. Real Estate – Investing in properties, either through direct ownership or real estate investment trusts (REITs), can offer steady income through rents and long-term appreciation.

4. Mutual Funds and ETFs – These investment vehicles pool money from multiple investors to buy a diversified portfolio of stocks, bonds, or other assets. They are an easy way to diversify without buying individual securities.

5. Commodities and Cryptocurrencies – These are more speculative investments that can provide high returns but carry significant risk. Commodities like gold, oil, and agricultural products or newer assets like Bitcoin can fluctuate drastically.

The Power of Compounding

One of the most significant advantages of investing is the power of compounding. Compounding refers to earning returns on your initial investment as well as the returns you've already earned. Over time, this can lead to exponential growth in your wealth.

Diversification: Don't Put All Your Eggs in One Basket

One of the most important principles of investing is diversification. Diversifying means spreading your investments across different asset classes and sectors to reduce risk. By not putting all your money into one stock, bond, or asset type, you can protect yourself from significant losses if one of your investments underperforms.

A diversified portfolio might include stocks from various industries, bonds from different issuers, real estate investments, and even a small allocation to alternative assets like precious metals or cryptocurrency. The idea is to balance your risk and reward by having a mix of investments that perform differently under various market conditions.

Setting Clear Investment Goals

Before you begin investing, it's important to have clear financial goals in mind. Are you saving for retirement? Do you want to buy a house in five years? Are you looking to build wealth for your children's education?

Your investment strategy should align with these goals. For example, if you're investing for retirement 30 years down the line, you can afford to take on more risk and invest in growth-oriented assets like stocks. On the other hand, if you're saving for a down payment on a house in the next few years, you might prefer safer, more liquid investments like bonds or a high-yield savings account.

Risk Tolerance and Time Horizon

Investing always involves risk, and it's crucial to understand your risk tolerance. Risk tolerance refers to your ability to withstand losses in your portfolio without panicking or making irrational decisions. Some people are comfortable with high-risk investments that can potentially yield higher returns, while others prefer more conservative investments that offer stability.

Your risk tolerance is also affected by your investment time horizon, or how long you plan to leave your money invested. If you're young and investing for the long term, you can afford to take on more risk because you have time to recover from market fluctuations. However, if you're closer to retirement, you might want to reduce your exposure to risky assets and focus on preserving your capital.

Dollar-Cost Averaging

One strategy that can help reduce the impact of market volatility is dollar-cost averaging. This involves consistently investing a fixed amount of money at regular intervals, regardless of market conditions. By doing so, you buy more shares when prices are low and fewer when prices are high, which helps to average out the cost of your investments over time.

For example, if you invest $500 every month in a stock or mutual fund, you'll end up purchasing more shares when prices are down and fewer shares when prices are high. This strategy can help reduce the risk of investing a lump sum of money at the wrong time, such as right before a market downturn.

Long-Term Focus

Investing is not a get-rich-quick strategy. The most successful investors are those who adopt a long-term perspective and avoid trying to time the market. While short-term market fluctuations are inevitable, history has shown that the stock market tends to rise over the long run.

By staying focused on your long-term goals and not reacting to short-term volatility, you can increase your chances of achieving consistent returns over time.

Automating Your Investments

One of the best ways to stay on track with your investment strategy is to automate your contributions. Many brokers and financial institutions offer automatic investment plans, allowing you to set up recurring contributions to your portfolio. By automating your investments, you can ensure that you stay disciplined, invest regularly, and take advantage of the power of compounding.

Automation also removes the emotional aspect of investing, making it less likely for you to make impulsive decisions during periods of market turbulence.

Evaluating Your Investments Regularly

While long-term investing is key, it's still important to periodically review your portfolio and make adjustments when necessary. This could involve rebalancing your portfolio to ensure your asset allocation remains aligned with your goals, risk tolerance, and time horizon. For example, if stocks have significantly outperformed bonds in your portfolio, you might need to sell some stocks and buy more bonds to maintain your desired balance.

It's also essential to stay informed about changes in the market and economic conditions. A well-informed investor is better equipped to make sound decisions and avoid panic when the market experiences downturns.

Smart investing is not about making risky bets or chasing the latest trends. It's about taking a disciplined, long-term approach to growing your wealth. By understanding the different types of investments, setting clear goals, diversifying your portfolio, and staying focused on the big picture, you can make your money work for you and achieve financial independence over time.

Remember, investing is a journey, and success comes with patience, consistency, and a willingness to learn. By following these principles, you can grow your wealth and achieve your financial dreams.

The Basics of Investing: Stocks, Bonds, and Mutual Funds

Investing is a powerful way to grow wealth over time, and it is important for anyone interested in financial independence to understand the basics of investing. Three of the most common investment vehicles are stocks, bonds, and mutual funds. These financial instruments provide opportunities for individuals to earn returns and build wealth. This article will introduce you to each of these investment options, providing a foundation to help you make informed decisions about your financial future.

Stocks: Ownership in a Company

When you purchase stocks, you are buying a small piece of ownership in a company. Stocks represent equity, meaning you own a share of the company and its assets. Public companies issue stocks to raise capital, and investors buy them in the hope that the company will grow and generate profits. As the company succeeds, the stock value may increase, and shareholders can sell their stocks for a profit.

Types of Stocks:

There are two main types of stocks: common stocks and preferred stocks.

1. Common Stocks:

Common stockholders are the basic owners of a company and have voting rights, which allows them to influence major corporate decisions. They also have the potential for dividend payouts, though these are not guaranteed. If the company performs well, the value of common stock can rise. However, common stockholders are last in line to be compensated if a company goes bankrupt, after bondholders and preferred stockholders.

2. Preferred Stocks:

Preferred stockholders are generally given priority over common stockholders when it comes to dividend payouts and in the case of bankruptcy. However, preferred stockholders do not have voting rights in the company. The downside is that preferred stocks often do not provide the same high growth potential as common stocks.

Risks and Rewards:

Stocks tend to offer higher returns than other investments over the long term, but they come with a higher level of risk. Stock prices can fluctuate wildly due to company performance, economic conditions, or global events. While the long-term trend has been upward, short-term volatility is common.

Bonds: A Loan to a Company or Government

Bonds are essentially loans made to companies, municipalities, or governments, and they are considered fixed-income securities because they pay interest at regular intervals, typically annually or semi-annually. In exchange for loaning their money, bondholders receive periodic interest payments, called the coupon, and the return of their principal amount when the bond matures.

Types of Bonds:

Bonds come in different forms depending on who issues them and the terms associated with them.

1. Government Bonds:

Government bonds are issued by national governments, such as U.S. Treasury bonds. These are considered low-risk investments because the government backs them. Investors are typically guaranteed interest payments, and the principal is returned when the bond matures.

2. Municipal Bonds:

Issued by local or state governments, municipal bonds are used to fund public projects such as infrastructure development or schools. Municipal bonds may offer tax advantages for certain investors, such as tax-exempt income in some cases.

3. Corporate Bonds:

Corporate bonds are issued by companies. They tend to offer higher interest rates than government bonds because they are riskier. The risk varies depending on the creditworthiness of the company issuing the bond.

Risks and Rewards:

Bonds are typically considered safer investments than stocks, particularly government bonds. However, they do not offer the same growth potential. The main risks associated with bonds are interest rate risk (the value of bonds decreases when interest rates rise), credit risk (the issuer defaults on payment), and inflation risk (the value of interest payments may not keep up with inflation).

Mutual Funds: A Pool of Investments

A mutual fund is an investment vehicle that pools money from many investors to invest in a diversified portfolio of stocks, bonds, or other assets. This allows investors to own a variety of securities with a single investment. Mutual funds are managed by professional fund managers who make decisions on behalf of the investors.

Types of Mutual Funds:

1. Equity Funds:

These funds primarily invest in stocks and aim to provide high returns through capital appreciation. They can be aggressive or conservative depending on the fund's strategy.

2. Bond Funds:

These funds primarily invest in bonds and focus on providing regular income through interest payments. Bond funds can be used for conservative investors seeking stability.

3. Index Funds:

Index funds are designed to mirror the performance of a specific market index, such as the S&P 500. These funds offer low fees and aim to track the market's overall performance, making them a good choice for long-term investors seeking broad market exposure.

4. Balanced Funds:

Balanced funds invest in a mix of stocks and bonds to provide a balance of growth and income. They are typically used by investors who want diversification and moderate risk.

Risks and Rewards:

Mutual funds provide diversification, which can reduce risk compared to investing in individual stocks or bonds. The fund's performance depends on the assets it holds, and returns vary based on market conditions. While mutual funds are less risky than individual stocks, they are still subject to market risk. The performance of the fund also depends on the skill of the fund manager.

Choosing the Right Investment for You

When choosing between stocks, bonds, and mutual funds, it's important to consider your investment goals, risk tolerance, and time horizon.

- Stocks are ideal for investors with a high risk tolerance and a long-term time horizon, seeking growth and capital appreciation.
- Bonds are better suited for conservative investors looking for steady income with less volatility. They are ideal for those approaching retirement or looking for lower-risk investments.
- Mutual Funds are a good choice for investors who want diversification but do not have the time or expertise to manage individual stocks or bonds. They can suit various risk profiles and investment goals.

Stocks, bonds, and mutual funds are the basic building blocks of a diversified investment portfolio. Each has its own unique characteristics, and understanding their differences is key to developing a successful investment strategy. By carefully considering your financial goals and risk tolerance, you can determine which combination of these investment vehicles will help you build wealth over time. Keep in mind that while investing always carries risk, informed decisions can lead to long-term financial success.

Long-term vs. Short-term Investing Strategies

When it comes to investing, two primary strategies dominate the field: long-term investing and short-term investing. Each approach carries its own set of risks, rewards, and unique benefits. Understanding the differences between these strategies is essential for investors looking to maximize their returns while managing their risk exposure. This section delves into the key distinctions between long-term and short-term investing, helping you make informed decisions about which strategy may be right for your financial goals.

Understanding Long-Term Investing

Long-term investing refers to the strategy of holding investments for an extended period, typically five years or more. The objective of this approach is to allow investments to appreciate over time, riding out the inevitable fluctuations in the market. The primary goal for long-term investors is to benefit from the compound growth of their investments and the overall upward trajectory of the market.

Benefits of Long-Term Investing

1. Compounding Returns: One of the greatest advantages of long-term investing is the power of compounding. As investments generate returns—whether in the form of interest, dividends, or capital gains—those returns are reinvested to generate even more returns over time. This compounding effect can significantly increase the value of your

investment portfolio over the years.

2. Lower Transaction Costs: Long-term investors generally make fewer trades, reducing the amount of money spent on commissions, fees, and other transaction-related costs. By holding investments over the long term, you avoid the costs of frequent trading associated with short-term strategies.

3. Riding Out Volatility: While short-term markets are often volatile, long-term investors are able to ride out these periods of instability. By staying invested over an extended period, they can take advantage of market recoveries and benefit from the overall upward trend of the economy.

4. Tax Benefits: In many countries, long-term capital gains are taxed at a lower rate than short-term capital gains. This tax advantage allows long-term investors to keep more of their returns, further increasing the profitability of their investments.

5. Lower Stress: Long-term investing generally requires less frequent monitoring of your investments. Investors are not concerned with daily market fluctuations, and they don't have to react quickly to sudden price changes. This can reduce the emotional stress that comes with constant trading.

Drawbacks of Long-Term Investing

1. Market Risk: While long-term investing allows for the potential of market recovery, it also exposes investors to the risk of long-term market downturns. A financial crisis or significant economic event could cause the value of an investment to drop sharply over many years,

potentially delaying or diminishing returns.

2. Less Flexibility: Once an investor commits to a long-term investment, it may be difficult to access those funds if they need liquidity in the short term. This lack of flexibility can be a significant disadvantage if an investor faces unforeseen financial difficulties.

Understanding Short-Term Investing

Short-term investing, as the name suggests, involves holding investments for a shorter duration, typically anywhere from a few days to a few years. Short-term investors aim to take advantage of price fluctuations in the market, aiming for quick profits by buying low and selling high. This strategy is often associated with higher levels of risk but can offer the potential for quicker returns.

Benefits of Short-Term Investing

1. Quick Returns: Short-term investing can provide investors with the opportunity to generate quick profits. By actively trading stocks or other financial instruments, short-term investors can capitalize on market volatility and earn returns over a short period of time.

2. Liquidity: Since short-term investments are held for brief periods, they generally offer higher liquidity than long-term investments. If an investor needs to access their funds quickly, they can sell their investments with relative ease.

3. Flexibility: Short-term investing allows for greater flexibility, as investors can quickly adjust their portfolios in response to market trends. For instance, if a short-term investor sees an emerging

opportunity, they can buy into the asset and take advantage of price movements without being tied to a long-term holding period.

4. Active Involvement: For those who enjoy actively managing their investments, short-term investing can be an engaging and rewarding strategy. Investors can track market news, monitor real-time price changes, and make decisions on the fly, all of which provide a dynamic approach to investing.

Drawbacks of Short-Term Investing

1. Higher Risk: Short-term investing often exposes investors to higher risks compared to long-term investing. Market fluctuations can be more extreme in the short term, and short-term investors must react quickly to avoid significant losses. Additionally, short-term price movements are often unpredictable, which makes it harder to anticipate the best time to buy or sell.

2. Increased Costs: Frequent trading incurs higher transaction costs, such as commissions, taxes, and fees. These additional expenses can significantly eat into the profits of short-term investors, making it harder to generate substantial returns, particularly for small-scale investments.

3. Stress and Time Commitment: Short-term investing requires constant attention to market trends and developments. This can be stressful and time-consuming, especially for those who are not full-time investors. The pressure to make quick decisions can lead to emotional decision-making, which may ultimately harm returns.

4. Tax Implications: In many countries, short-term capital gains are

taxed at a higher rate than long-term capital gains. This means that short-term investors may pay more in taxes on their profits, reducing the overall profitability of their strategy.

Comparing Long-Term and Short-Term Investing

While both long-term and short-term investing offer distinct advantages, they also come with unique challenges. The choice between thc two depends largely on an investor's goals, risk tolerance, and time horizon.

- Risk Tolerance: Long-term investing tends to be less risky, as investors can ride out market volatility over time. Short-term investing, on the other hand, requires a higher risk tolerance, as price fluctuations can be dramatic in the short term.

- Time Horizon: Long-term investing is ideal for those who are looking to grow their wealth over an extended period, such as for retirement. Short-term investing, however, may be suitable for individuals seeking more immediate returns or those who have a shorter time frame for achieving their financial goals.

- Active vs. Passive Involvement: If you enjoy actively managing your investments and staying on top of market trends, short-term investing may be more suited to your preferences. Long-term investing, however, allows for more passive management, with less frequent adjustments and a focus on steady, gradual growth.

Both long-term and short-term investing offer viable pathways for growing wealth, but they are designed for different types of investors with varying financial goals. Long-term investing emphasizes steady growth over time, relying on the power of compounding and market recoveries, while short-term investing seeks to capitalize on immediate market trends and price fluctuations.

Your choice between the two strategies should depend on factors such as your risk tolerance, financial goals, time horizon, and the amount of time you can commit to monitoring the markets. Some investors may even choose to blend both strategies, using long-term investments to build a stable foundation and short-term investments to seize more immediate opportunities.

Ultimately, the key to success in either strategy is discipline, knowledge, and careful planning. By understanding the pros and cons of each approach, you can craft an investment strategy that aligns with your unique goals and financial situation.

Risk Management and Understanding Your Tolerance for Risk

Investing in financial markets inherently involves a degree of risk. However, not all risks are created equal, and understanding your own tolerance for risk is a critical factor in creating a successful investment strategy. By managing risk effectively and knowing how much risk you are willing to take, you can align your investments with your long-term financial goals and reduce the chances of making emotionally driven decisions during market fluctuations.

What Is Risk Tolerance?

Risk tolerance refers to the level of uncertainty or potential financial loss you are willing and able to endure while investing. It varies from person to person based on factors such as age, financial goals, investment experience, and emotional capacity to handle market volatility. It is essential to understand your own risk tolerance because it helps determine the types of investments that are best suited for you, whether they are low-risk, moderate-risk, or high-risk investments.

Types of Risk

Before diving into how to manage risk, it's important to understand the different types of risk that can affect investments:

1. Market Risk: This refers to the risk of investments losing value due to factors affecting the entire market, such as economic downturns, political instability, or changes in interest rates. It is generally considered unavoidable but can be mitigated through diversification.

2. Credit Risk: This type of risk applies to fixed-income investments, like bonds, and occurs when an issuer defaults or is unable to meet its financial obligations.

3. Liquidity Risk: Liquidity risk arises when an investor is unable to sell an investment quickly enough or at a reasonable price. Investments in less liquid assets, like real estate or certain types of stocks, can expose you to this risk.

4. Inflation Risk: Inflation risk occurs when the return on an investment fails to outpace inflation, causing the purchasing power of your returns to decline over time.

5. Interest Rate Risk: This type of risk primarily affects fixed-income securities like bonds. When interest rates rise, the value of existing bonds falls, leading to a decline in the bondholder's investment value.

Assessing Your Risk Tolerance

Several factors influence your risk tolerance, including:

1. Age: Younger investors may have a higher risk tolerance because they have more time to recover from market fluctuations. Older investors approaching retirement tend to have a lower risk tolerance to avoid jeopardizing their retirement savings.

2. Investment Goals: Your financial goals also influence your risk tolerance. For example, if you're investing for long-term growth and can afford to ride out market volatility, you might be willing to take on more risk. Conversely, if you need your money in the short term, you'll likely prefer less risky, more stable investments.

3. Income and Financial Stability: Those with a steady income and sufficient emergency savings tend to have a higher risk tolerance. Investors with unstable income or minimal savings might prefer safer investments that preserve their capital.

4. Experience and Knowledge: Your experience and understanding of financial markets play a role in how much risk you're willing to take. Investors who have a better grasp of market dynamics and risk management strategies are generally more comfortable with higher-risk investments.

5. Emotional Capacity: Risk tolerance is not just about financial capacity—it's also about your emotional ability to handle volatility. Some investors are emotionally comfortable with market fluctuations, while others may panic during market downturns. Your emotional resilience will help determine your ideal level of risk.

Managing Risk in Investing

Once you understand your risk tolerance, the next step is to develop a strategy to manage risk effectively:

1. Diversification: Diversifying your investments across different asset classes, sectors, and geographical regions is one of the most effective ways to reduce risk. By holding a mix of investments, the impact of a downturn in one asset class may be offset by gains in another.

2. Asset Allocation: This refers to how you distribute your investments across different asset types, such as stocks, bonds, real estate, and cash. The right asset allocation depends on your risk tolerance and investment goals. A more aggressive investor might allocate a larger percentage to stocks, while a conservative investor may favor bonds and cash.

3. Rebalancing: Over time, the value of your investments will change, causing your asset allocation to shift. Regularly rebalancing your portfolio—typically once or twice a year—can help maintain the level of risk you're comfortable with and ensure that your investments remain aligned with your goals.

4. Dollar-Cost Averaging: This strategy involves investing a fixed amount of money at regular intervals, regardless of market conditions. This approach reduces the risk of making large investments at the wrong time and can smooth out market volatility over the long term.

5. Hedging: Hedging involves using financial instruments like options or futures to protect your portfolio from adverse market movements. While it's often used by more advanced investors, hedging can be a

valuable tool for managing risk.

6. Emergency Fund: Building an emergency fund is a critical risk management tool. Having liquid savings in place for unexpected life events or market downturns can provide peace of mind and prevent the need to sell investments during unfavorable times.

Adjusting Risk Tolerance Over Time

Your risk tolerance may evolve over time as your financial situation, goals, and emotions change. It's important to reassess your tolerance periodically, especially after significant life events such as marriage, having children, career changes, or nearing retirement. If your risk tolerance decreases, you can adjust your portfolio to become more conservative, shifting towards less volatile assets like bonds or cash.

Understanding and managing your risk tolerance is fundamental to building a successful investment strategy. By evaluating your financial goals, personal circumstances, and emotional comfort with risk, you can make more informed decisions that help you achieve long-term financial success. Remember that risk is inherent in investing, but with a thoughtful approach, you can minimize it and maximize your potential for growth.

Building Wealth Through Passive Income

Building wealth is a goal many of us aspire to, but it often seems out of reach, requiring hard work, constant effort, and time. However, one of the most efficient ways to build long-term wealth is through passive income—earnings generated with minimal effort or active involvement once the initial setup is in place. Passive income can provide a steady stream of revenue while allowing you to focus on other areas of your life. This article will discuss different types of passive income, how to get started, and how you can use them to build wealth over time.

What is Passive Income?

Passive income refers to money earned with little to no effort on a regular basis after an initial investment of time, money, or effort. Unlike active income, where you trade your time directly for money (e.g., through a salaried job or freelance work), passive income allows you to earn money while you sleep, travel, or focus on other pursuits. It is the key to achieving financial independence and wealth over time.

The Importance of Passive Income

The importance of passive income cannot be overstated. Having multiple income streams can help you mitigate the risk of financial instability caused by losing a job or facing an unexpected crisis. Moreover, it allows you to generate income even when you are not actively working. By building passive income, you increase your financial security, which is essential in today's volatile economy.

The true power of passive income lies in compounding. For example, if you invest in rental properties or dividend-paying stocks, your money begins to generate more income, which can be reinvested to generate even greater returns. Over time, these investments can significantly grow your wealth.

Different Types of Passive Income

1. Real Estate Investments

Real estate is one of the most reliable sources of passive income. Purchasing rental properties allows you to earn rental income on a monthly basis. In addition, the property's value may increase over time, offering potential capital gains when sold. Real estate investment trusts (REITs) are another option for those who prefer to invest in property without the hassle of managing physical real estate. REITs allow investors to pool their money into property investments and earn returns in the form of dividends.

2. Dividend Stocks

Dividend stocks are another excellent source of passive income. Companies that generate substantial revenue often share a portion of that revenue with their shareholders in the form of dividends. By investing in stocks with a history of consistent dividend payouts, you can build a passive income stream over time. Moreover, dividend stocks often increase in value over time, allowing you to accumulate wealth while earning regular dividends.

3. Peer-to-Peer Lending

Peer-to-peer lending platforms such as LendingClub or Prosper enable individuals to lend money directly to others in exchange for interest payments. This is a form of passive income because once you've made the loan, you will receive regular interest payments over time. Peer-to-peer lending carries some risks, but with proper research, it can be a profitable way to earn passive income.

4. Online Businesses and Digital Products

The digital era has brought about opportunities for creating passive income through online businesses and digital products. For example, if you create and sell online courses, e-books, or digital art, you can continue earning money without active involvement once the products are created. A website or e-commerce platform can be monetized through affiliate marketing, sponsored content, or selling products, generating passive income over time. Similarly, apps or SaaS (software-as-a-service) models allow you to generate income continuously while the systems run on autopilot.

5. Affiliate Marketing

Affiliate marketing involves promoting products or services for other companies in exchange for a commission. You can promote products through your website, blog, or social media platforms. Once you have a following or audience, affiliate links embedded in your content can generate ongoing income with little additional effort. Affiliate marketing is especially popular among bloggers, YouTubers, and influencers who can reach large audiences.

6. Creating an E-commerce Business

Another option is creating an online store that sells physical products. While this may require significant effort upfront, once your business is established and you have an automated system in place for processing orders, the ongoing management can be minimal. By utilizing fulfillment services such as Amazon FBA (Fulfilled by Amazon), you can sell products while Amazon handles the storage, packing, and shipping of the goods.

7. Royalties from Intellectual Property

If you have creative talents, you can earn passive income from royalties on intellectual property such as books, music, artwork, or patents. For instance, authors can receive royalties from the sale of their books or e-books, musicians can earn royalties from music streaming platforms, and artists can license their artwork for use in commercials or products. These royalty payments continue for as long as the work is being used.

Steps to Building Passive Income

1. Invest Time and Capital Wisely

Building a passive income stream requires an initial investment of time and/or capital. If you're investing in real estate, you may need to put up money for a property, while investing in dividend stocks might require initial capital as well. For creating digital products or building an online business, the upfront work could include content creation, website development, and marketing efforts. Be patient as these income streams take time to build.

2. Diversify Your Investments

One of the keys to building wealth through passive income is diversification. Rather than putting all your money into a single source of passive income, spread your investments across multiple income streams. This will not only help you manage risk but also ensure that you have multiple ways of generating income. For example, you might choose to invest in dividend stocks, real estate, and peer-to-peer lending to maximize your earning potential.

3. Reinvest Your Earnings

In the early stages of building passive income, it's important to reinvest your earnings. Whether from rental income, dividends, or royalties, reinvesting the profits you make will allow you to grow your income over time. By continually reinvesting your earnings, you create a snowball effect where your money works for you and produces increasingly larger returns.

4. Monitor Your Investments

While passive income is designed to require minimal effort, it doesn't mean you can ignore your investments entirely. Keep track of the performance of your income streams and make adjustments as needed. Regularly reviewing your investments helps you stay on top of market changes, economic conditions, and potential risks.

Building wealth through passive income is an achievable goal for anyone willing to invest time, money, and effort upfront. Whether through real estate, stocks, digital products, or affiliate marketing, passive income offers the opportunity to build long-term wealth while requiring minimal day-to-day involvement. By diversifying your investments, reinvesting your earnings, and staying committed to your financial goals, you can build a steady and reliable source of passive income that will help you achieve financial freedom.

How to Invest in Building Multiple Streams of Income

In today's fast-paced financial world, the idea of relying on a single income source has become increasingly risky. Whether you're a salaried worker, entrepreneur, or freelancer, the landscape of job security and economic shifts can leave anyone vulnerable. Building multiple streams of income is not just a smart way to safeguard your finances; it's also a proactive step towards achieving long-term wealth and financial freedom.

Multiple streams of income allow you to diversify your financial portfolio, minimize risks, and create new opportunities for growth. Below are some key steps on how to strategically invest in building multiple streams of income.

1. Assess Your Current Financial Situation

Before you begin adding streams of income to your life, it's essential to assess your current financial standing. Take a deep dive into your income, expenses, debts, and savings. This will help you understand where you stand financially and provide insight into how much you can realistically invest into building new income streams.

Ask yourself the following questions:

- What are my current sources of income?
- What are my fixed and variable expenses?
- Do I have any debt, and what is the interest rate?
- How much can I save or invest each month toward a new income source?

By answering these questions, you'll have a clear starting point and be able to make informed decisions as you move forward.

2. Start with Passive Income Streams

Passive income refers to the money you earn with minimal ongoing effort. This is one of the most efficient ways to create multiple income streams. With the right investment, you can generate a steady flow of income without having to trade your time for money continuously.

Some popular passive income streams to consider are:

- Real Estate Investment: Purchasing rental properties or investing in real estate investment trusts (REITs) can yield passive income. Rent from tenants or dividends from REITs can generate a steady stream of cash flow.

- Dividend Stocks: Dividend-paying stocks are shares of companies that distribute a portion of their profits to shareholders. If you invest in the right companies, you could receive regular dividends without needing to sell the stock.

- Peer-to-Peer Lending: Platforms such as LendingClub and Prosper allow you to lend money to individuals or small businesses and earn interest as they repay their loans.

- Creating Digital Products: Consider creating and selling digital products such as e-books, online courses, or stock photography. Once created, these products can be sold repeatedly, providing passive income over time.

3. Diversify with Active Income Streams

While passive income is crucial for long-term wealth, active income is still an important part of your overall strategy. Active income requires more time and effort but can be highly rewarding in the short term.

Examples of active income streams include:

- Freelancing: Offer your skills and expertise on platforms such as Upwork, Fiverr, or Freelancer. This could include writing, graphic design, marketing, web development, or consulting.

- E-commerce: Selling products online through platforms like Amazon, eBay, or Etsy can generate substantial income. You can either source products to sell or create your own (like hand-crafted goods or digital products).

- Affiliate Marketing: Promote other people's products or services on your blog, social media, or website. You can earn a commission for every sale made through your referral links.

- Coaching or Consulting: If you have experience or expertise in a particular field, you could offer coaching or consulting services to individuals or businesses.

4. Leverage Your Existing Skills and Network

When building multiple streams of income, leveraging your existing skills and network can accelerate the process. Think about how you can utilize your talents or knowledge to create additional income streams that require minimal investment.

For example:

- Teaching or Tutoring: If you have proficiency in a specific subject or field, you can offer tutoring or teaching services in person or online through platforms like VIPKid or Teachable.

- Public Speaking: If you're comfortable speaking in front of an audience, you can build a career as a motivational speaker or a subject matter expert, earning fees for events and conferences.

- Networking: Building and nurturing a strong network of professionals can open doors for new business opportunities, partnerships, and collaborations that provide additional streams of income.

5. Invest in Yourself

Your knowledge, skills, and mindset are some of your most valuable assets. The more you invest in your personal growth and development, the better equipped you'll be to build and manage multiple income streams.

Consider the following steps:

- Education: Take courses, read books, and attend seminars that teach you how to manage money, build wealth, and scale businesses.

- Develop New Skills: Learn new skills that are in high demand, such as coding, digital marketing, graphic design, or financial management. Upskilling will make you more marketable and open up new income opportunities.

- Mindset Development: A growth mindset is essential when it comes to creating and sustaining multiple streams of income. Focus on building resilience, adaptability, and discipline.

6. Set Clear Financial Goals and Track Your Progress

When building multiple streams of income, setting clear financial goals is crucial for staying focused and motivated. Make sure to establish short-term and long-term goals for each income stream.

For example:

- Short-term goal: "I want to earn $500 per month from my freelance writing work within the next 6 months."

- Long-term goal: "I want to have three rental properties generating a total of $5,000 in passive income within the next 5 years."

Track your progress regularly, and adjust your strategies as needed to stay on course. Financial planning tools, apps, or spreadsheets can help you stay organized and measure your success.

7. Be Patient and Consistent

Building multiple income streams takes time and effort. The key is consistency. While some streams will start generating income immediately, others may take months or even years before they become profitable.

The most successful individuals in the world didn't become wealthy overnight. They built multiple income streams step by step, consistently reinvesting their earnings and diversifying their financial portfolios.

Creating multiple streams of income is one of the best ways to secure your financial future. By diversifying your sources of revenue, you can protect yourself from economic fluctuations, job insecurities, and unexpected expenses. Whether you start with passive income or build your way up through active income, the goal is to create a system that works for you and allows you to achieve financial independence. By following the steps outlined above, you can start your journey toward financial freedom and long-term wealth.

Invest wisely, stay disciplined, and always be open to new opportunities that come your way.

The Power of Compound Interest in Growing Savings

When it comes to building wealth, many people look for ways to maximize their savings over time. One of the most powerful yet often overlooked tools in growing wealth is compound interest. While interest itself is a familiar concept to most people, understanding how compound interest works—and its potential to accelerate wealth accumulation—can significantly impact the way you approach savings and investment decisions.

What is Compound Interest?

At its core, compound interest is the interest on a loan or deposit that is calculated based on both the initial principal and the accumulated interest from previous periods. In simpler terms, compound interest allows you to earn interest on the interest you've already earned, creating a snowball effect where your money grows exponentially over time. This differs from simple interest, where interest is calculated only on the original principal amount.

To illustrate this, consider a savings account that earns 5% interest annually. With simple interest, you would earn 5% of your initial deposit each year. For example, if you invested $1,000, you would earn $50 in interest each year, bringing your total balance to $1,050 after the first year, and so on.

In contrast, with compound interest, the interest earned each year is added to the principal, and in the following year, you earn interest not just on your original deposit but also on the interest that has already accumulated. This means your interest grows faster, as it compounds over time.

How Compound Interest Works

To better understand the power of compound interest, let's break down the process step by step:

1. Initial Investment: You start by depositing a sum of money into a savings or investment account. This is your principal.
2. Interest Earned: Over time, your investment earns interest. With compound interest, this interest is added back into your account.
3. Next Interest Period: In the next period, your investment earns interest not just on your original principal but also on the interest from previous periods.

The Impact of Time

The power of compound interest is most apparent when you allow your investments to grow over a long period. The longer your money remains invested, the more significant the effects of compounding. This is because, over time, the interest begins to generate more interest, leading to exponential growth.

Let's consider the following example. If you invested $1,000 in an account that compounds annually at a rate of 5%, here's how your investment would grow over the years:

- After 10 years: $1,628.89
- After 20 years: $2,653.30
- After 30 years: $4,321.94

As you can see, the longer you let your money grow, the more it compounds. In the first few years, the growth might seem relatively modest, but over time, it accelerates. This is one of the key reasons why starting to save and invest early can lead to significant wealth accumulation over a lifetime.

The Role of Interest Rates

While time is a critical factor in the power of compound interest, the interest rate also plays an important role. The higher the interest rate, the faster your money will grow. However, it's important to note that interest rates can vary depending on where you invest your money. For instance, a savings account at a bank might offer a lower interest rate compared to a stock investment, but it comes with lower risk.

When it comes to compound interest, even small changes in the interest rate can have a significant effect on your final balance over time. Let's use the same $1,000 principal, but this time let's compare two interest rates: 5% and 10%. Here's how the investment would grow over 30 years at each rate:

- At 5% interest: $1,000 becomes $4,321.94 after 30 years.
- At 10% interest: $1,000 becomes $17,449.40 after 30 years.

The difference is remarkable. This illustrates why it's important to not only start investing early but to also look for investments that offer higher returns, such as stocks or mutual funds, while being mindful of the associated risks.

Compound Interest in Different Timeframes

While the examples above illustrate the growth of compound interest over long periods, it's important to recognize that compound interest also works on a smaller scale. Even if you're only saving for a few years or months, compound interest can still help you grow your savings.

The Importance of Consistency

In addition to starting early and choosing higher interest rates, consistency is a crucial element of using compound interest to your advantage. Regularly contributing to your investment or savings account can significantly accelerate your progress.

For instance, if you invest $100 every month into a retirement account that compounds monthly at a 5% annual rate, the compounded returns will be even more substantial over time. Not only does your principal grow, but the recurring contributions add more fuel to the compounding process.

In the case of monthly contributions, after 30 years, your investment would be significantly larger compared to a one-time $1,000 investment, even though both earn the same interest rate. This highlights the power of regular saving in addition to compound interest.

Risks and Considerations

While compound interest is a powerful tool for growing wealth, it's essential to recognize that all investments come with some level of risk. Interest rates aren't always guaranteed, especially in the case of stock investments or high-yield savings accounts. Additionally, inflation can erode the real value of your returns over time. It's crucial to consider these factors when choosing how to invest your money.

Moreover, different financial products and institutions may have varying compounding periods—some may compound interest daily, while others compound it quarterly or annually. The more frequently interest is compounded, the faster your investment will grow.

The power of compound interest lies in its ability to generate exponential growth over time. By starting early, investing regularly, and taking advantage of higher interest rates, you can watch your savings grow at an impressive pace. However, it's important to be mindful of the risks and to make informed investment decisions. With patience and consistency, compound interest can become one of the most powerful tools in your wealth-building journey, helping you achieve your financial goals faster than you may have ever imagined.

Financial Planning for the Future

Financial planning is an essential part of life that helps individuals navigate their financial goals, secure their futures, and manage their resources effectively. Whether you're planning for retirement, saving for a home, or setting aside funds for your children's education, effective financial planning allows you to make informed decisions and develop a strategy that aligns with your long-term aspirations. Financial planning provides you with a roadmap that ensures that you're prepared for any financial challenges that may arise in the future.

Why Financial Planning is Important

Many people avoid financial planning because it can seem overwhelming or tedious. However, without a well-thought-out plan, it can be easy to mismanage resources, accumulate debt, or fail to reach personal financial goals. The importance of financial planning lies in its ability to offer clarity, reduce financial stress, and provide a solid foundation for the future. Planning ahead ensures that your money is working for you, even when you're not actively managing it. It allows you to anticipate potential obstacles and prepare accordingly.

The future is unpredictable, but with solid financial planning, you can prepare for the unknown and maintain control over your finances. It also helps you feel more confident about the decisions you make and enables you to achieve both short-term and long-term goals.

The Key Steps in Financial Planning

1. Set Clear Goals

The first step in financial planning is to define your financial goals. Ask yourself, "What do I want to achieve financially in the next five, ten, or even twenty years?" Your goals will determine the strategies and tools you'll use to manage your finances. Common goals include:

- Saving for retirement
- Buying a home or paying off a mortgage
- Building an emergency fund
- Paying for your children's education
- Paying off debt

Once you know your goals, break them down into smaller, achievable milestones. This will help you stay focused and motivated as you work toward your larger objectives.

2. Create a Budget

A budget is one of the most powerful tools for financial planning. It allows you to track your income and expenses, providing you with a clear picture of where your money is going. By creating a detailed budget, you can identify areas where you may be overspending and adjust accordingly.

A well-structured budget will typically consist of:

- Income: Your salary, business income, passive income, or any other earnings.
- Fixed Expenses: Rent or mortgage, utilities, insurance, and other regular expenses.
- Variable Expenses: Groceries, entertainment, transportation, and other flexible spending.
- Savings: Set aside a portion of your income for long-term savings or investments.

Tracking your spending habits will also give you insight into your financial health and enable you to make more informed decisions about managing your money.

3. Build an Emergency Fund

Unexpected events, such as medical emergencies or job loss, can disrupt your financial stability. That's why it's important to set aside an emergency fund, which serves as a financial cushion for unforeseen circumstances. Most financial experts recommend saving at least three to six months' worth of living expenses in an easily accessible account, such as a high-yield savings account.

Having an emergency fund provides peace of mind and protects you from accumulating high-interest debt when emergencies arise.

4. Reduce and Manage Debt

Debt can significantly affect your financial well-being and hinder your ability to build wealth. A crucial part of financial planning is managing and reducing debt. Start by prioritizing high-interest debt, such as credit card balances, which can quickly accumulate interest.

Consider the following debt-reduction strategies:

- The Debt Snowball Method: Pay off your smallest debts first, then use the money you were paying toward those debts to pay off the next smallest debt. This method builds momentum as you eliminate one debt after another.
- The Debt Avalanche Method: Pay off high-interest debts first, which can save you money in interest over time.
- Consolidating Debt: If you have multiple loans or credit cards, consider consolidating them into one loan with a lower interest rate to reduce your overall payments.

Eliminating debt is a long-term process, but taking control of it will free up more money for saving and investing.

5. Invest for the Future

Investing is one of the most effective ways to grow your wealth over time. By investing in stocks, bonds, real estate, or other financial instruments, you allow your money to generate returns, which can compound over time.

Consider the following investment options:

- Retirement Accounts: Contribute to tax-advantaged retirement accounts, such as a 401(k) or IRA, to save for the future while enjoying tax benefits.
- Stock Market: Investing in individual stocks, mutual funds, or exchange-traded funds (ETFs) allows you to diversify your portfolio

and potentially earn higher returns.

- Real Estate: Purchasing property or investing in real estate funds can help you build wealth through capital appreciation and rental income.

The key to successful investing is long-term consistency. The earlier you start, the more you benefit from compound interest and market growth.

6. Plan for Retirement

Retirement may seem far off, but the earlier you begin saving, the more comfortable your future retirement will be. In addition to saving through retirement accounts, such as a 401(k) or IRA, it's important to estimate how much money you'll need in retirement and develop a strategy to reach that goal.

To calculate your retirement needs, consider factors such as:

- Your desired retirement age
- Your expected lifestyle and expenses in retirement
- The rate of return on your investments
- Inflation rates

A retirement plan should be tailored to your unique needs and should be revisited regularly to ensure that it stays on track.

7. Seek Professional Advice

While you can manage many aspects of your finances independently, there may be times when you need professional guidance. Financial advisors, accountants, or wealth managers can help you create an investment plan, optimize your taxes, and ensure that you're making the best financial decisions for your future.

When choosing a financial advisor, make sure to check their qualifications, experience, and reputation. A good advisor will help you navigate complex financial matters and offer tailored advice based on your goals.

Financial planning is a vital practice that ensures long-term financial stability, wealth accumulation, and peace of mind. By setting clear goals, creating a budget, building an emergency fund, reducing debt, investing wisely, planning for retirement, and seeking professional advice, you can secure your financial future and achieve financial freedom.

Remember, financial planning is not a one-time event but an ongoing process. Life circumstances change, and so should your financial plans. By staying proactive and committed to your financial goals, you will pave the way for a prosperous and secure future.

Retirement Savings Strategies: 401(k), IRA, and Other Options

Retirement planning is crucial for ensuring that you have a stable and comfortable future. Saving for retirement can seem overwhelming, but with the right strategies and an understanding of available options, you can make smarter decisions that align with your long-term financial goals. Two of the most common retirement savings vehicles are the 401(k) and the Individual Retirement Account (IRA). These accounts come with specific benefits and tax advantages, and they serve as the foundation for retirement plans for millions of Americans. But beyond these two, there are other strategies to consider in your quest for financial freedom in your golden years.

1. Understanding the 401(k)

The 401(k) is one of the most popular retirement plans, especially for those who work in the corporate world. Named after the section of the tax code that governs it, the 401(k) allows employees to contribute a portion of their salary to a retirement fund, where the contributions grow tax-deferred until withdrawal. Employers often match contributions, making it a great way to build wealth for retirement.

Contribution Limits

In 2023, the contribution limit for a 401(k) plan is $22,500 for individuals under 50 years of age. For those 50 and older, you can make a "catch-up" contribution of up to $7,500, bringing the total contribution to $30,000.

Employer Match

One of the most attractive aspects of a 401(k) is the employer match. Many employers will match a certain percentage of your contributions, which can significantly boost your retirement savings.

Tax Benefits

Contributions to a 401(k) plan are made pre-tax, which lowers your taxable income in the current year. For instance, if you contribute $5,000 to your 401(k), you only pay taxes on $45,000 instead of $50,000 if that was your salary. This tax advantage can make a significant impact on your ability to save, especially in the early years of your career.

The taxes are due when you begin taking withdrawals, typically after age 59½, at which time the withdrawals are taxed as ordinary income.

Investment Options

401(k) plans often offer a limited number of investment options, typically mutual funds, target-date funds, and index funds. While these may offer solid returns, the limited selection means you have less flexibility in terms of diversification compared to other investment vehicles.

2. Understanding the IRA (Individual Retirement Account)

An IRA is another popular retirement savings option. It functions similarly to a 401(k) but is not tied to an employer. This makes it ideal for individuals who are self-employed or those who want to have more control over their retirement savings. There are two main types of IRAs: Traditional IRAs and Roth IRAs.

Traditional IRA

A traditional IRA allows you to contribute pre-tax money to an account that grows tax-deferred until retirement. The contribution limit in 2023 is $6,500, or $7,500 if you're 50 or older.

Tax Benefits: Contributions to a Traditional IRA are tax-deductible in the year they are made, reducing your taxable income for that year. Like a 401(k), the funds grow tax-deferred until withdrawal, at which point they are taxed as ordinary income.

Income Limits: The ability to deduct contributions to a Traditional IRA is phased out at certain income levels, particularly if you or your spouse is covered by a workplace retirement plan.

Roth IRA

The Roth IRA is a powerful tool for retirement planning due to its tax structure. Unlike a Traditional IRA, contributions to a Roth IRA are made with after-tax money. However, when you withdraw funds during retirement, they are tax-free, as long as you've held the account for at least five years and are 59½ or older.

Income Limits: Roth IRAs have income limits. In 2023, individuals with a modified adjusted gross income (MAGI) over $138,000 ($218,000 for married couples) are ineligible to contribute directly to a Roth IRA.

Flexibility: Roth IRAs also offer more flexibility than Traditional IRAs. You can withdraw your contributions at any time without penalty or taxes, though withdrawing earnings before 59½ can result in taxes and penalties.

3. Health Savings Accounts (HSAs)

An often-overlooked tool for retirement savings is the Health Savings Account (HSA). While this account is primarily designed for healthcare expenses, it also offers excellent benefits for retirement planning.

HSAs allow you to contribute pre-tax money to an account, grow those funds tax-deferred, and, when used for qualified medical expenses, withdraw the funds tax-free. After age 65, you can withdraw the funds for non-medical expenses without penalty, though you will be taxed as if it were a regular IRA withdrawal.

In 2023, you can contribute up to $3,850 for individual coverage and $7,750 for family coverage, with a $1,000 catch-up contribution for those 55 and older. HSAs can be an excellent way to save for medical expenses in retirement while enjoying some of the same benefits as retirement-focused accounts.

4. Employer-Sponsored Retirement Plans for Self-Employed Individuals

If you're self-employed, you may not have access to a traditional 401(k), but there are retirement plans designed specifically for self-employed individuals. Two popular options are the Solo 401(k) and the SEP IRA (Simplified Employee Pension).

Solo 401(k)

A Solo 401(k) allows business owners to contribute both as an employer and as an employee. In 2023, you can contribute up to $22,500 as an employee and an additional employer contribution of up to 25% of your income, up to a total of $66,000 (or $73,500 if you're 50 or older).

SEP IRA

A SEP IRA is a retirement plan for self-employed individuals or small business owners that allows for much higher contribution limits than a Traditional or Roth IRA. In 2023, you can contribute up to 25% of your income, with a maximum of $66,000.

5. Other Strategies for Retirement Savings

While the 401(k) and IRAs are the most common retirement accounts, there are several other strategies and accounts that may complement your retirement plan.

- Taxable Investment Accounts: These accounts are not specifically designed for retirement but can be used to invest in stocks, bonds, and mutual funds. They offer no tax advantages, but there is no limit on how much you can contribute or withdraw. They provide flexibility and liquidity, making them useful for supplementing other retirement savings.

- Annuities: An annuity is a financial product that provides a stream of income in retirement. You can purchase an annuity through an insurance company, which will then pay you a fixed amount for a specific period or for the rest of your life. While not suitable for everyone, annuities can provide guaranteed income and stability.

Building a successful retirement savings strategy requires planning, discipline, and an understanding of your financial situation. The 401(k) and IRA are the foundational tools for many individuals' retirement plans, offering tax benefits and the potential for long-term growth. Other accounts, such as the HSA, SEP IRA, or taxable investment accounts, can be used to complement and enhance your retirement savings strategy.

No matter which retirement plan you choose, the most important thing is to start saving as early as possible, regularly contribute, and make smart, well-informed decisions about your financial future. By making use of the various retirement savings strategies available, you can set yourself up for a secure and comfortable retirement.

The Importance of Life Insurance and Estate Planning

Life insurance and estate planning are essential components of a comprehensive financial strategy. Many people, however, fail to understand their significance, often putting them off until it's too late. These two elements work hand-in-hand to secure not only the financial future of your family but also provide peace of mind knowing that your affairs are in order. In this article, we'll delve into why life insurance and estate planning are critical and how they play a vital role in your long-term financial security.

What is Life Insurance?

At its core, life insurance is a contract between the policyholder and the insurance company, where the company agrees to provide a sum of money to beneficiaries upon the policyholder's death. In exchange, the policyholder pays regular premiums. While life insurance primarily exists to provide a financial safety net for loved ones, it also offers benefits during the policyholder's lifetime, depending on the type of life insurance selected.

Life insurance ensures that loved ones—typically a spouse, children, or other dependents—are financially supported in the event of an unexpected death. The death benefit can be used to cover funeral expenses, pay off outstanding debts like mortgages, credit cards, or student loans, and replace lost income, allowing the surviving family members to maintain their quality of life.

Types of Life Insurance

There are several types of life insurance, each designed to meet specific needs. The most common are term life insurance and permanent life insurance.

- Term Life Insurance: This type of life insurance provides coverage for a specific period (usually 10, 20, or 30 years). If the policyholder dies within this term, the beneficiaries receive the death benefit. Term life insurance is generally more affordable but doesn't build cash value, meaning it offers coverage only during the term's duration.

- Whole Life Insurance: A form of permanent insurance, whole life provides lifelong coverage and builds a cash value that can be borrowed against or withdrawn. Whole life policies are more expensive but offer a guaranteed death benefit, making them an appealing choice for long-term coverage.

- Universal Life Insurance: This type is also permanent but is more flexible than whole life insurance. It allows policyholders to adjust their premiums and death benefits and offers the opportunity to accumulate cash value. Universal life insurance is often considered a hybrid between term and whole life policies.

Why Is Life Insurance Important?

1. Income Replacement: The primary purpose of life insurance is to replace lost income. If the primary income earner in a family were to unexpectedly pass away, life insurance can help ensure that the family can still meet living expenses without significant financial strain. It can replace the income lost due to death, allowing dependents to continue their lifestyle without drastic changes.

2. Debt Repayment: In addition to income replacement, life insurance can also provide the funds needed to pay off outstanding debts. For example, if the policyholder passes away with a mortgage, car loans, or credit card debt, the life insurance payout can help clear those liabilities, so the surviving spouse or children are not burdened with them.

3. Funeral and End-of-Life Costs: The cost of a funeral, including burial or cremation services, memorials, and any related expenses, can be significant. Life insurance can cover these costs, sparing family members from the financial burden of such expenses during an already emotionally challenging time.

4. Wealth Building: Some types of life insurance, like whole and universal life insurance, allow policyholders to accumulate cash value over time. This can be borrowed against or used as a supplemental savings account for retirement, offering an additional financial benefit.

What is Estate Planning?

Estate planning refers to the process of organizing and managing your assets to ensure that they are distributed according to your wishes after you pass away. A comprehensive estate plan includes a variety of legal documents designed to ensure your assets are transferred smoothly, minimize estate taxes, and avoid complications for your heirs. Some of the most common elements of estate planning include wills, trusts, and power of attorney.

The Key Components of Estate Planning

1. Wills: A will is a legal document that dictates how a person's assets and property should be distributed after their death. It can also specify guardianship arrangements for minor children, ensuring that your children will be cared for by someone you trust. A will helps streamline the probate process and minimize potential disputes among family members.

2. Trusts: Trusts are legal arrangements that allow a trustee to hold

and manage assets on behalf of the beneficiaries. Trusts can help minimize estate taxes, avoid the lengthy probate process, and ensure that assets are distributed according to the wishes of the deceased. There are several types of trusts, including revocable trusts (which can be modified during the grantor's lifetime) and irrevocable trusts (which cannot be changed once established).

3. Power of Attorney: This legal document grants someone the authority to make decisions on your behalf in the event that you become incapacitated. There are two types of power of attorney: medical and financial. A medical power of attorney gives someone the authority to make healthcare decisions for you, while a financial power of attorney grants someone the authority to manage your financial affairs.

4. Living Wills: A living will provides instructions about your health-care preferences, including end-of-life care. It can specify whether or not you want life-sustaining treatments in certain situations, ensuring that your wishes are followed if you become unable to communicate them yourself.

Why Is Estate Planning Important?

1. Control Over Asset Distribution: Without an estate plan, your assets will be distributed according to state laws, which may not align with your wishes. By creating a will or trust, you can ensure that your belongings, property, and finances go to the people or organizations you care about most.

2. Minimize Family Disputes: When a person passes away without a clear estate plan, family members may fight over who gets what, leading to unnecessary conflict and tension. Having an estate plan in

place provides clear guidance, reducing the potential for disputes and ensuring that your loved ones are not burdened with ambiguity during an already difficult time.

3. Tax Benefits: Proper estate planning can help minimize estate taxes and ensure that your heirs receive the maximum benefit from your assets. Trusts, in particular, can be used to reduce the taxable value of your estate and protect assets from high estate taxes.

4. Plan for Incapacity: Estate planning isn't only about preparing for death; it's also about preparing for the possibility of becoming incapacitated. With the proper power of attorney and living will, you can ensure that someone you trust will be able to make important medical and financial decisions on your behalf.

Both life insurance and estate planning are critical components of a comprehensive financial strategy. Life insurance ensures that your loved ones are financially supported after your death, while estate planning gives you the control to dictate how your assets are distributed, who will care for your children, and what medical decisions will be made in the event of incapacity. By putting these two strategies in place, you can protect your family's financial future and ensure that your legacy lives on in the way you intend.

Taking the time to understand the importance of life insurance and estate planning—and putting them into action—provides invaluable peace of mind for you and your loved ones, allowing you to navigate life's uncertainties with confidence and security.

How to Leave a Financial Legacy for Your Family

Leaving a financial legacy is about more than just passing down money—it's about setting your loved ones up for a prosperous future. Whether you're building a legacy through saving, investing, or simply imparting wisdom, the goal is to ensure your family can thrive long after you're gone. Here's a step-by-step guide on how to leave a meaningful financial legacy for your family.

1. Establish Clear Financial Goals

Before you can leave a legacy, it's essential to have a clear understanding of what you want to achieve. Are you focused on saving for your children's education, helping them with a down payment for a home, or providing a comfortable retirement for them? Start by identifying specific goals for your family's financial future.

Writing these goals down can make them feel more attainable. Prioritize your objectives, keeping in mind both short-term and long-term aspirations, and ensure you align them with your values. A well-planned legacy is one that is intentional, not left to chance.

2. Create a Will and Estate Plan

Having a will is one of the most important steps in leaving a financial legacy. It ensures that your assets—whether property, investments, or savings—are distributed according to your wishes. Without a will, your estate may go through probate, a lengthy and costly process, during which the state decides how your assets are distributed.

Estate planning also involves setting up trusts, powers of attorney, and designating beneficiaries for things like life insurance or retirement accounts. Trusts, for example, can provide a tax-efficient way to transfer assets to your heirs and give you control over when and how your beneficiaries receive their inheritance.

By creating a comprehensive estate plan, you ensure that your financial wishes are carried out with minimal complications.

3. Invest in Education and Financial Literacy

One of the best ways to leave a legacy is to equip your family with the knowledge to manage their finances wisely. Financial education is an investment that pays dividends. Start by teaching your children or loved ones the basics of budgeting, saving, investing, and managing debt.

Consider setting up educational funds, such as 529 college savings plans for your children or grandchildren, to help with future educational expenses. If your loved ones are financially literate, they'll be able to take care of the wealth you've passed down and continue building on it for generations to come.

In addition to formal education, you can invest in resources such as books, seminars, or courses that promote financial literacy. Encourage ongoing learning about financial strategies and decision-making. You want them to not only benefit from your legacy but to continue growing it.

4. Create a Strong Investment Portfolio

An essential part of leaving a financial legacy is ensuring that you've accumulated wealth through prudent investing. Whether it's through stocks, bonds, real estate, or businesses, your investments play a crucial role in creating the foundation of your financial legacy.

Start by saving a portion of your income regularly. Take advantage of retirement accounts like 401(k)s and IRAs, which provide tax advantages. Diversifying your investments across different asset classes will help protect your wealth and ensure that it grows consistently over time.

Remember, the earlier you begin investing, the better. Compound interest works best when given time to grow, which means that the sooner you start investing, the more substantial your legacy will be for future generations.

Additionally, real estate investments can be an effective way to build long-term wealth. Whether you buy property to rent or purchase a vacation home, owning real estate can provide both steady income and long-term value appreciation.

5. Consider Life Insurance

Life insurance can be a powerful tool for leaving a financial legacy. If you were to pass away unexpectedly, life insurance could ensure your family is financially secure, providing them with the resources needed to pay off debts, cover funeral expenses, and maintain their lifestyle.

Term life insurance provides coverage for a specific period and can be more affordable, while whole life insurance offers lifetime coverage and accumulates cash value over time. By including life insurance as part of your estate planning strategy, you ensure your loved ones are financially protected, no matter what happens.

Additionally, life insurance policies can be used as an inheritance for your children or grandchildren, providing them with a lump sum to invest, start a business, or use for any other financial need.

6. Minimize Taxes for Your Heirs

Taxes can diminish the value of your estate, which is why tax planning should be an integral part of your strategy. Estate taxes, inheritance taxes, and capital gains taxes can erode the wealth you've worked hard to build.

Work with a financial planner or tax professional to develop a strategy that minimizes the tax burden on your heirs. This might involve setting up a trust, making use of tax-free gift allowances, or spreading out your wealth over time through strategic gifting. The goal is to pass down as much of your estate as possible without triggering unnecessary taxes.

7. Encourage a Giving Mentality

Another aspect of leaving a legacy is teaching your loved ones the importance of giving back. Charitable giving can be a significant part of your legacy, whether it's in the form of donating to causes that align with your values or setting up a family foundation.

Charitable giving doesn't just benefit the recipients; it also provides your family with the opportunity to carry on your legacy of generosity. Consider allocating a portion of your estate to charities, creating a donor-advised fund, or establishing a scholarship for future generations. This sets a powerful example of selflessness and community involvement.

8. Maintain Open Communication with Your Family

Financial discussions are often difficult to have, but open and honest communication about money is crucial to ensure your legacy is preserved. Having conversations about your plans, financial goals, and your estate can help your family understand your wishes, manage expectations, and avoid confusion after your passing.

Don't hesitate to talk to your loved ones about the importance of preserving and growing the legacy you've built. Provide them with the tools they need to manage wealth responsibly, and ensure they understand how to make sound financial decisions.

9. Leave a Legacy Beyond Money

While money and assets are important, don't forget that your true legacy also consists of the values, lessons, and experiences you pass down to your family. Encourage them to focus on personal development, happiness, and health. Teach them about integrity, hard work, and the importance of relationships.

You can create a legacy that lasts far beyond financial wealth by imparting wisdom, building strong family bonds, and inspiring future generations to live fulfilling lives. This kind of emotional and spiritual inheritance will be just as important—and often more enduring—than the financial wealth you pass down.

Leaving a financial legacy is a way to ensure that your family remains financially secure and empowered, long after you're gone. The legacy you leave doesn't have to be huge, but it should be intentional. By setting clear goals, investing in education, creating an estate plan, and maintaining open communication, you can provide a foundation for your loved ones to build upon. A legacy, both financial and otherwise, has the power to shape the lives of generations to come, allowing them to live with greater opportunities, security, and happiness.

Your financial legacy is not just about what you leave behind—it's about how you prepare the next generation to continue growing, thriving, and making a positive impact.

Staying Consistent and Committed

Saving money is often easier said than done. Whether it's for an emergency fund, a big purchase, or simply building wealth, consistency and commitment are key components to long-term financial success. Without them, it's easy to slip back into old habits or become distracted by life's inevitable curveballs. However, with the right strategies in place, staying committed to saving can become a part of your daily life. Let's explore how to remain consistent and committed to your financial goals, as well as how to overcome obstacles that may come your way.

The Importance of Consistency in Saving

When it comes to building financial security, consistency is everything. Saving small amounts consistently over time can often yield greater results than sporadic, large deposits. Even if your budget only allows for $20 a week, that's still $1,040 a year, and it's a lot easier to stick with this small, achievable amount than to try to save a large lump sum all at once. Over time, these small contributions add up, and your financial goals start to feel more attainable.

Consistent saving creates a habit. Just like brushing your teeth or exercising regularly, the more you incorporate savings into your routine, the easier it becomes. This can help make saving feel less like a sacrifice and more like an integral part of your life. The key is to automate the process as much as possible.

Automating Your Savings

One of the most effective ways to stay consistent is to automate your savings. This means setting up regular, automatic transfers from your checking account to your savings account. By doing this, you're ensuring that saving happens without having to think about it. This is particularly important because human behavior often leans toward spending rather than saving. When we see money sitting in our checking accounts, it's easy to spend it on impulse buys or short-term desires. However, when that money is automatically moved to a savings account, it's less likely to be touched.

You can set up automated transfers through your bank's online portal or by contacting your bank directly. Choose an amount that fits within your budget, whether that's weekly, bi-weekly, or monthly. By treating savings like any other monthly expense, you're more likely to commit to it. Plus, the money will be out of sight and out of mind, making it less tempting to dip into it for non-essential purchases.

Setting Realistic and Achievable Goals

Having clear goals is another essential part of staying consistent with saving money. If you don't have a reason to save, it can be difficult to stay committed to your efforts. Setting specific, realistic, and time-bound goals can provide the motivation needed to continue saving.

For instance, rather than saying, "I want to save money," set a goal like "I want to save $3,000 in the next year for a vacation" or "I want to save three months' worth of living expenses for an emergency fund." These goals give you something tangible to work toward, making the process feel more purposeful.

Start with smaller goals that are easier to achieve. Once you've hit one target, you can move on to bigger goals. Achieving small victories along the way will give you the confidence and momentum to continue saving and help you avoid feeling overwhelmed by your larger objectives.

Tracking Your Progress

Tracking your savings progress is an excellent way to stay motivated and committed. Regularly monitoring how much you've saved will provide a sense of accomplishment and will also give you a clear picture of where you stand in relation to your goals. There are numerous apps and tools that can help you track your savings, such as Mint, YNAB (You Need A Budget), or even basic spreadsheets.

When you see your balance growing, it reinforces the idea that your efforts are paying off, which can make it easier to stay committed. You'll also be able to evaluate whether you're on track to meet your goals or if adjustments need to be made to your savings plan.

Accountability and Support

Sometimes, staying consistent can be challenging, and that's when accountability comes into play. If you're struggling to stay committed to your savings, it can help to have someone to check in with, whether it's a friend, partner, or even a financial advisor. Sharing your goals with others can make you feel more responsible for following through on them, and it can also give you someone to turn to for encouragement when the going gets tough.

If you have a partner, work together to create a joint savings plan and hold each other accountable. Couples who share financial goals and support each other in their efforts often find greater success in saving money.

Another option is to join an online community, such as a personal finance forum or social media group, where you can discuss your savings journey with others who share similar goals. These communities offer encouragement, advice, and motivation, and knowing that others are on the same journey can help you stay committed to your own.

Overcoming Obstacles

Despite your best efforts, there will likely be times when your commitment to saving money is tested. Life is full of unexpected expenses—car repairs, medical bills, or other emergencies—that may make it seem impossible to continue saving. During these times, it's important to remember that setbacks don't mean failure. Instead, view them as temporary hurdles to overcome. The key is to remain adaptable and persistent.

If you're faced with an emergency that depletes your savings, don't give up entirely. Instead, readjust your goals and create a plan to replenish the funds. It might take longer than you initially planned, but as long as you keep your eye on the prize, you can get back on track.

Another obstacle that may arise is burnout. It's easy to get discouraged when you don't see immediate results, especially if your savings goals are significant. Remember that building wealth is a long-term process, and progress may be slow at times. The important thing is that you're moving forward, even if it's at a steady pace. Keeping your long-term goals in mind and staying patient will help you stay consistent, even when the results aren't immediate.

Make Saving Enjoyable

Finally, one of the most important aspects of staying committed to saving money is to make the process enjoyable. While it may seem counterintuitive, finding ways to enjoy the journey can help you stay motivated.

Consider treating yourself once you reach certain milestones. For example, after saving 50% of your goal, you might reward yourself with a small treat—something that doesn't undo your progress but still makes you feel appreciated for your hard work.

If you can, make saving feel like a game. Challenge yourself to save a little bit more each month, or create mini-goals to help break down your larger target. The more fun you can make the process, the easier it will be to stay consistent.

Staying consistent and committed to saving money is not always easy, but it's an essential habit for financial success. By automating your savings, setting clear goals, tracking your progress, seeking accountability, and remaining adaptable in the face of obstacles, you can build a strong foundation for financial stability. With time, your commitment will pay off, and your savings will grow. Remember, even small steps add up over time, and consistency is the key to achieving your financial dreams.

How to Stay Motivated and Avoid Burnout

Saving money is a crucial step towards achieving financial independence, building a safety net, and securing a better future. However, it's not always easy to stay motivated, especially when it feels like the goal is far away, or the process is dragging on for too long. It's common to hit a roadblock or even feel burnt out while saving. The key to staying on track is to find ways to stay motivated without letting the pursuit of financial goals overwhelm you. Below are practical steps that will help you stay motivated while saving money and avoid burnout in the process.

1. Set Clear, Achievable Goals

One of the primary reasons people lose motivation when saving money is that they set vague or overly ambitious goals. When you don't have a clear target, it becomes difficult to track progress and celebrate small wins. Instead, break your savings goals into smaller, manageable pieces.

For instance, rather than simply saying, "I want to save more," consider setting specific amounts you want to save each month and a realistic timeframe for achieving each goal. Whether it's building an emergency fund of $1,000 within the next six months or saving for a vacation, having a defined and measurable goal helps you focus your efforts.

It's also helpful to prioritize your goals. Save for an emergency fund first, then move on to other savings goals like retirement or large purchases. This approach allows you to make steady progress without feeling overwhelmed.

2. Track Your Progress

Once you have set clear goals, it's essential to track your progress. Seeing how far you've come can be incredibly motivating. Use a budgeting app, a simple spreadsheet, or even a good old-fashioned journal to monitor your savings. Tracking your progress also allows you to celebrate small victories along the way, which can help you maintain enthusiasm.

Consider creating a visual tracker, such as a progress bar or a savings thermometer. This kind of visual representation can be a fun and effective way to stay engaged with your goal.

3. Find Meaning and Purpose in Your Savings Journey

To stay motivated, connect your savings goals with something meaningful to you. Whether it's buying your dream home, traveling the world, or simply achieving peace of mind knowing that you have money set aside for emergencies, tying your goal to a deeper sense of purpose will keep you going when times get tough.

If you understand why you are saving, the process becomes much more enjoyable. Think of it as investing in your future self. Every small sacrifice now is one step closer to your ultimate goal, and that can help provide the motivation to push through moments of doubt.

4. Create a Budget and Stick to It

A solid budget is one of the most effective ways to stay on track with your savings. By clearly defining your income and expenses, you can identify areas where you can cut back and allocate more towards your savings goals.

It's important to be realistic about your budget. Trying to save too much too soon might lead to frustration and burnout. Start by saving a small percentage of your income, and as your savings grow, gradually increase the amount. Over time, this will build momentum.

Moreover, having a budget allows you to recognize unnecessary spending habits and reduce them, ensuring that you can save more without feeling deprived.

5. Celebrate Small Wins

Staying motivated doesn't mean waiting until you reach your final goal to celebrate. It's essential to acknowledge small victories along the way. For example, celebrate when you reach the halfway point of your emergency fund or when you manage to save a few hundred dollars in a month. These celebrations will help you recognize how much progress you've made and provide the motivation to keep going.

The key to avoiding burnout is to find balance. Rewarding yourself occasionally (without going overboard) keeps the journey enjoyable and sustainable.

6. Avoid Extreme Sacrifices

While saving money is important, it's also important to avoid over-restriction. If you are constantly cutting back on your spending, you may start to feel deprived, which can lead to burnout. Instead of making extreme sacrifices, try finding a balance between saving and enjoying life.

For example, if you are saving for a vacation, allow yourself to occasionally indulge in a small treat, like a coffee out with a friend, without feeling guilty. Moderation is key to keeping the process enjoyable and sustainable. Also, avoid adopting the mindset of "I can't afford anything"—this mentality only leads to frustration. Instead, focus on mindful spending.

7. Automate Your Savings

Automating your savings is one of the easiest ways to ensure that you consistently save without the effort of thinking about it every time you get paid. Set up automatic transfers from your checking account to your savings account, so you're saving without having to actively remember to do it.

This method ensures that saving becomes part of your routine and removes the temptation to spend the money you've planned to save. With automation, it becomes easier to save consistently, and over time, you'll notice your savings grow.

8. Find Support in Others

Saving money can sometimes feel like a lonely journey, especially if you're surrounded by people who aren't focused on their finances. One way to avoid burnout is to find a support system. Whether it's a friend, family member, or an online community, having someone to share your progress with and who can motivate you on tough days can make all the difference.

You can even join groups or social media communities focused on saving and budgeting. Sharing tips, celebrating wins, and offering advice to others can keep you engaged with your savings goal and provide the emotional boost you need when you feel like giving up.

9. Remember to Review and Adjust

Life happens, and sometimes your circumstances may change. It's crucial to periodically review your savings plan and make adjustments as needed. If you experience a temporary setback, such as a decrease in income, don't feel like all is lost. Instead, reassess your goals and adjust your plan accordingly.

Sometimes, adjusting your savings plan or taking a break can help you stay on track and prevent feelings of burnout.

10. Be Patient and Give Yourself Grace

Finally, one of the most important things to remember is that financial freedom is a marathon, not a sprint. Be patient with yourself, and give yourself grace when you face setbacks. Saving money is a long-term process that requires dedication, but it's not about perfection.

You may have moments where you slip up and spend more than you planned or feel discouraged when you don't reach your goal as quickly as you hoped. Don't let these moments derail your efforts. Stay focused, and give yourself credit for the progress you've already made.

Staying motivated while saving money is possible with the right strategies in place. The key is to set realistic, clear goals, track your progress, stay connected to the bigger picture, and avoid making drastic sacrifices that could lead to burnout. Saving money is a journey, and by staying focused, patient, and positive, you can achieve your financial goals without losing sight of what matters most. Stay committed, and remember that every small step counts toward creating a better financial future.

www.ingramcontent.com/pod-product-compliance
Lightning Source LLC
LaVergne TN
LVHW052323200926
848481LV00002B/655

* 9 7 9 8 2 3 0 8 0 7 7 1 1 *